John Habberton

The Barton experiment

John Habberton

The Barton experiment

ISBN/EAN: 9783743303348

Manufactured in Europe, USA, Canada, Australia, Japa

Cover: Foto ©Suzi / pixelio.de

Manufactured and distributed by brebook publishing software
(www.brebook.com)

John Habberton

The Barton experiment

THE

BARTON EXPERIMENT

BY THE AUTHOR OF "HELEN'S BABIES"

J.H. Habberton

———

NEW YORK

G. P. PUTNAM'S SONS

182 FIFTH AVENUE

1877

PREFACE.

THIS book is not offered to the public as a finished romance, or even as an attempt at one;
the persons who appear on its pages are not only
not those who inspire pretty stories, but they are
so literally the representatives of individuals who
have lived that they cannot well be separated from
their natural surroundings. It has seemed to the
author that if American people could behold some
of the men who have astonished themselves and
others by their success as reformers, individual
effort would not be so rare in communities where
organization is not so easily effected, and where
unfortunates are ruined in the midst of their neighbors, while organization is being hoped for. It is
more than possible, too, that the accepted business
principle that the pocket is the source of power, is
not as clearly recognized as it should be in reform
movements, and that the struggles of some of the

characters outlined herein may throw some light upon this unwelcome but absolute fact.

The ideal reformer, the man of great principles and eloquent arguments, fails to appear in these pages, not because of any doubts as to his existence, but because his is a mental condition to which men attain without much stimulus from without, while it need not be feared that in the direction of individual effort and self-denial, the greatest amount of suggestion will ever urge any one too far.

CONTENTS.

THE

BARTON EXPERIMENT.

CHAPTER I.

REFORMERS AT WHITE HEAT.

L ONG and loud rang all the church bells of Barton on a certain summer evening twenty years ago. It was not a Sunday evening, for during an accidental lull there was heard, afar off yet distinctly, the unsanctified notes of the mail-carrier's horn. And yet the doors of the village stores, which usually stood invitingly open until far into the night, were now tightly closed, while the patrons of the several drinking-shops of Barton congregated quietly within the walls of their respective sources of inspiration, instead of forming, as was their usual wont, lively groups on the sidewalk.

The truth was, Barton was about to indulge in a

monster temperance meeting. The "Sons of Temperance," as well as the "Daughters" and "Cadets" thereof, the "Washingtonians," the "Total Abstinence Society," and all various religious bodies in the village had joined their forces for a grand demonstration against King Alcohol. The meeting had been appropriately announced, for several successive Sundays, from each pulpit in Barton; the two schoolteachers of Barton had repeatedly informed their pupils of the time and object of the meeting; the "Barton Register" had devoted two leaders and at least a dozen items to the subject; and a poster, in the largest type and reddest ink which the "Register" office could supply, confronted one at every fork and crossing of roads leading to and from Barton, and informed every passer-by that Major Ben Bailey, the well-known champion of the temperance cause, would address the meeting, that the "Crystal Spring Glee Club" would sing a number of stirring songs, and that the Barton Brass Band had also been secured for the evening. The only inducement which might have been lacking was found at the foot of the poster, in the two words, "Admittance Free."

No wonder the villagers crowded to the Methodist Church, the most commodious gathering-place in the town. Long before the bells had ceased clanging the church was so full that children occupying full seats were accommodatingly taken on the laps of their parents, larger children were lifted to the window-sills, deaf people were removed from the pews to the altar steps, and chairs were brought from the various residences and placed in the aisles. Outside the church, crowds stood about near the windows, while more prudent persons made seats of logs from the woodpile which the country members of the congregation had already commenced to form against the approaching winter.

A sudden hush of the whispering multitude ushered in the clergy of Barton, and, for once, the four reverend gentlemen really seemed desirous of uniting against a common enemy instead of indulging in their customary quadrangular duel. Then, amid a general clapping of hands, the members of the Crystal Spring Glee Club filed in and took reserved seats at the right of the altar; while the Barton Brass Band, announced by a general shriek of " Oh!" from all the children present, seated themselves on a raised platform on the left.

Squire Tomple, the richest and fattest citizen of

the town, was elected chairman, and accepted with a benignant smile. Then the Reverend Timotheus Brown, the oldest pastor in the village, prayed earnestly that intemperance might cease to reign. Squire Tomple then called on the band for some instrumental music, which was promptly given and loudly applauded, after which the Crystal Spring Glee Club sang a song with a rousing chorus. Then there was a touching dialogue between a pretended drunkard and his mother, in which the graceless youth was brought to a knowledge of the error of his ways, and moved to make a very full and grammatical confession. Then the band played another air, and the Glee Club sang " Don't you go, Tommy," and there was a tableau entitled " The First Glass," and another of "The Drunkard's Home," after which the band played still another air. Then a member of the Executive Committee stepped on tiptoe up to the chairman and whispered to him, and the chairman assumed an air of dignified surprise, edged expectantly to one side of his chair, and finally arose suddenly as another member of the Executive Committee entered the rear door arm-in-arm with the great Major Ben Bailey himself.

The committee-man introduced the Major to the

chairman, who in turn made the Major acquainted with the reverend clergy; the audience indulged in a number of critical and approving glances and whispers, and then the chair announced that the speaker of the evening would now instruct and entertain those there present. The speaker of the evening cleared his throat, took a swallow of water, threw his head back, thrust one hand beneath his coat-tails, and opened his discourse.

He was certainly a very able speaker. He explained in a few words the nature of alcohol, and what were its unvarying effects upon the human system; proved to the satisfaction and horror of the audience, from reports of analyses and from liquor-dealers' handbooks, that most liquors were adulterated, and with impure and dangerous materials; explained how the use of beer and light wines created a taste for stronger liquors; showed the fallacy of the idea that liquor was in any sense nutritious; told a number of amusing stories about men who had been drunk; displayed figures showing how many pounds of bread and meat might be bought with the money spent in the United States for liquor, how many comfortable homes the same money would build, how many suits of clothing it would pay for, how many churches it would erect, and how soon it would pay the National Debt (which in those days was foolishly considered large enough to be talked about). Then, after drawing a touching picture of the drunkard's home, and dramatically describing the horrors of the drunkard's death, the gallant Major made an eloquent appeal to all present to forsake forever the poisonous bowl, and dropped into his seat amid a perfect thunder of applause.

The lecture had been a powerful one; it was evident that the speaker had formed a deep impression on the minds of his hearers, for when the pledge was circulated, men and women who never drank snatched it eagerly and appended their names, some parents even putting pencils into baby fingers, and with devout pride helping the little ones to trace their names. Nor were the faithful alone in earnestness, for a loud shout of " Bless the Lord ! " from Father Baguss, who was circulating one of the pledges, attracted attention to the fact that the document was being signed by George Doughty, Squire Tomple's own book-keeper, one of the most promising young men in Barton, except that he occasionally drank. Then the list of names taken in the gallery was read, and it was ascertained that Tom Adams, who drove the brick-yard wagon, and whose sprees were mighty in length and magnitude, had also signed. Half a dozen men hurried into the gallery to congratulate Tom Adams, and so excited' that gentleman that he took a pledge and a pencil, went into the crowd outside the church, and soon returned with the names of some of the heaviest drinkers in town.

The excitement increased. Cool-headed men—men who rarely or never drank, yet disapproved of binding pledges—gave in their names almost before they knew it. Elder Hobbedowker moved a temporary suspension of the circulation of the pledges until the Lord could be devoutly thanked for this manifestation of his grace ; then the good elder assumed that his motion had been put and carried, and he immediately made an earnest prayer. During the progress of the prayer the leader of the band—perhaps irreverently, but acting under the general excitement—brought his men to attention, and the elder's "Amen" was drowned in the opening crash of a triumphal march. Then the Glee Club sang "Down with Rum," but were brought to a sudden stop by the chairman, who excused himself by making the important announcement that their fellow-citizen, Mr. Crupp, who had been a large vender of intoxicating beverages, had declared his intention to abandon the business forever. The four pastors shook hands enthusiastically with each other; while, in response to deafening cheers, the heroic Crupp himself was thrust upon the platform, where, with a trembling voice and a pale though determined face, he reaffirmed his decision. Old Parson Fish hobbled to the front of the pulpit, straightened his bent back until his mien had at once some of the lamb and the lion about it, and, raising his right hand authoritatively, started the doxology, " Praise God from whom all blessings flow," in which he was devoutly and uproariously joined by the whole assemblage. This done, the people, by force of habit, waited a moment as if expecting the benediction; then remembering it was not Sunday, they broke into a general and very enthusiastic chat, which ceased only when the sexton, who was a creature of regular habits, announced from the pulpit that the oil in the lamps would last only a few minutes longer, and that *he* had promised to be at home by ten o'clock.

Squire Tomple took the arm of the penitent

Crupp and appropriated him in full. There was a great deal to Squire Tomple besides avoirdupois, and when thoroughly aroused, his enthusiasm was of a magnitude consistent with his size. Besides, Squire Tomple was in the habit of having his own way, as became the richest man in Barton, and he appropriated Mr. Crupp as a matter of course. With Mr. Crupp on his arm and the great cause in his heart, he appeared to himself so fully the master of the situation that the foul fiend of drunkenness seemed conquered forever, and the Squire swung his cane with a triumphal violence which seriously threatened the safety of the villagers in front of and behind him.

The Squire held his peace while surrounded by the home-going crowd, as rightly became a great man; but when he had turned into the street in which Mr. Crupp lived, he said, with due condescension,

"Crupp, you've done the right thing; you *might* have done it sooner, but you can do a great deal of good yet."

The ex-rumseller quietly replied,

"Yes, if I'm helped at it."

"Helped? Of course you'll be helped, if you

1*

pray for it. You've repented; now address the throne of grace, and——"

"Yes, I know," interrupted Mr. Crupp. "I'm not entirely unacquainted with the Lord, if I *have* sold rum. You know his sun shines on the just and the unjust, and I've had a good share of it. It's help from men that I want, and am afraid that I can't get it."

"Why, Crupp," remonstrated the Squire, "you must have made something out of your business, if it *is* an infernal one."

"I don't mean that," replied Mr. Crupp, a little tartly. "You've been on your little drunks when you were young, of course?"

The Squire almost twitched Mr. Crupp off the sidewalk, as he exclaimed, with righteous indignation,

"I never was drunk in my life."

"Oh!" said the convert. "Well, some have, and pledges won't quiet an uneasy stomach, no way you can fix 'em. Them that never drank are all right, but the drinking boys that signed to-night'll be awful thirsty in the morning."

"Well," said the Squire, "*they* must pray, and act like men."

"Some of 'em don't believe in prayin', and some of 'em can't act like men, because 'tisn't in 'em. There's men that seem to need whisky as much as they need bread; leastways, they don't seem able to do without it."

"If I'd been you, and believed that, Crupp," replied the Squire, with noticeable coolness and deliberation, "I wouldn't have signed the pledge; that is, I wouldn't have stopped selling liquor."

"P'r'aps not," returned the ex-rumseller; "but with me it's different. There's some men that b'lieves that sellin' a woman a paper of pins, and measurin' out a quart of tar for a farmer, is small business, an' beneath 'em, but they stick to it. Now I believe I'm too much of a man to sell whisky, so I've stopped."

The Squire took the rebuke in silence; however much his face may have flushed, there were in Barton no tell-tale gas-lamps to make his discomfort visible. The Squire had grown rich as a vender of the thousand little things sold in country stores; he had many a time declared that storekeeping was a dog's life, and that he, Squire Tomple, was everybody's nigger—but he made no attempt to change his business.

"What I mean," continued Mr. Crupp, "by need-in' help, is this: I know just about how much every drinkin' man in town takes, an' when he takes it, an' about when he gets on his sprees. Now, if there's anybody to take an interest in these fellows at such times, they're going to have plenty of chances mighty soon."

CHAPTER II.

BUSINESS *vs.* PHILANTHROPY.

ON the morning after the meeting the happiest man in all Barton was the Reverend Jonas Wedgewell. He had been one of the first to agitate the subject of a grand temperance demonstration; in fact, he had, while preaching the funeral sermon of a young man who had been drowned while drunk, prophesied that the sad event which had on that occasion drawn his hearers together would give a mighty impetus to the temperance movement; then like a sensible, matter-of-fact prophet, he exerted himself to the uttermost that his prophecy might be fulfilled. He subscribed liberally to the fund which paid for advertising the meeting; he labored personally a full hour with the performer on the big drum, and ended by persuading him to forego a coon-hunt on that particular night, that he might take part in a hunt for nobler game. The Reverend Jonas had drafted all the pledges which were circulated during the meeting, and had seen to it that they contained no weak or ungrammatic expressions which might tempt thirsty souls to treat disrespectfully the documents and the principles they embodied. He had reached the church door at the third tap of the bell, had greeted all his reverend brethren with a hearty shake with both his own hands, and had offered the Reverend Timotheus Brown so many pertinent suggestions as to the prayer which that gentleman had been requested to make that the ancient divine remarked, with a touch of saintly sarcasm, that he did not consider that the occasion justified him in making a departure from his habit of offering strictly original prayers.

Through the whole course of the meeting good Pastor Wedgewell sat expectantly on the extreme end of the pulpit sofa, his body inclined a little forward, his hands upon his knees, his eyes gleaming brightly through polished glasses, and his whole pose suggesting the most intense earnestness. He discerned a telling point before its verbal expression was fully completed, his hands commenced to applaud the moment the point was announced; his varnished boots and well-stored head beat time alike to " Lily Dale," the march from " Norma," " Sweet

Spirit, hear my prayer," and such other airs as the band was not ashamed to play in public ; he sprang from his seat and approvingly patted the youthful backs of the pretended drunkard and his mother, he laughed almost hysterically at the wit of the lecturer, and moistened handkerchief after handkerchief as the able speaker depicted the sad results of drunkenness.   While the pledges were being circulated, the reverend man occupied a position which raked the house, and he was the first to announce to the faithful in the front seats the capture of any drinking man.   He intercepted Tom Lyker, a tinshop apprentice, who had signed the pledge, in the aisle, immediately after the audience was dismissed, and suggested that they should together hold a season of prayer in the study attached to the church ; and the rather curt manner in which the repentant but not altogether regenerate Thomas declined the invitation did not abash the holy man in the least ; for, as the audience finally dispersed, he secured a few faithful ones, with whom he adjourned to the study, and enjoyed what he afterward referred to as a precious season.

Mrs. Wedgewell, who rendered but feeble reverence unto him who was at once her spouse and her

spiritual adviser, had been known to say that when
the old gentleman was wound up there was no knowing when he would run down again; and all who
saw the good man on the morning after the meeting,
admitted that his wife's simile was an uncommonly
apt one. Squire Tomple believed so fully in the
advantages of the early bird over all others in search
of sustenance, that his store was always opened at
sunrise; yet George Doughty had just taken the
third shutter from the front window, when a gentle
tap on the shoulder caused him to drop the rather
heavy board upon his toes. As he wrathfully turned
himself, he beheld the approving countenance and
extended congratulatory hand of the Reverend
Wedgewell.

"George, my dear, my noble young friend," said
he, as the irate youth squeezed his agonized toes,
" you have performed a most noble and meritorious
action—an action which you will never have cause
to regret."

For a moment or two the young man's face said
many things not seemly to express in appropriate
words to a clergyman; but he finally recovered his
sense of politeness, and replied:

"I hope I shan't repent of it, but I don't know.

It may be noble and meritorious to sign the pledge, but a fellow needs to have twenty times as much man in him to keep it."

" Now you don't mean to say, George, that you'll allow such a vile appetite to regain its ascendency over you ? " pleaded the preacher.

"'*Tisn't* a vile appetite," quickly replied the young man. "I need whisky as much as I need bread and butter—yes, and a great deal more, too. I have to open the store at sunrise, and keep it open till nine o'clock and after, have to make myself agreeable to anywhere from two to twenty people at a time, sell all I can, watch people who will steal the minute your eye is off of them, not let anybody feel neglected, and see that I get cash from every-body who isn't good pay. When there isn't any-body here, I've got to keep the books, see that the stock don't run down in spots, and stir up peo-ple that are slow pay. The only way I can do it all is by taking something to help me. I *hate* whisky—I'm going to try to leave it alone; but I tell you, Dominie, it's going to be one of the big-gest fights you ever knew a young man to go into."

The reverend listener was as easily depressed as he was exalted, and Doughty's short speech had the

effect of greatly elongating the minister's countenance. Yet he had a great deal of that pertinacity
which is as necessary to soldiers of the cross as it is
to those of the bayonet; so he began manfully to
search his mind for some weapon or means of defense which the clerk could use. Suddenly his
countenance brightened, his benevolent eyes enlarged behind his glasses, and he exclaimed:

"Just the thing! My dear young friend, the
hand of Providence is in this matter. Your worthy
employer was the chairman of our meeting last
night; certainly he will be glad to give you such
assistance as shall lessen the amount of your labors.
Here he comes now. Let *me* manage this affair; I
really ask it as a favor."

"I'm much obliged, but I think—confound it!"
ejaculated the young man, as his companion has-
tened out of earshot and buttonholed Squire Tomple.
Half smiling and half frowning Doughty retired
from the door, but took up a new position, from
which he could see the couple. To the eyes of the
clerk, his employer seemed a rock in his unchanging
pose, while the old preacher, rich in many a grace
not peculiar to country storekeepers, yet utterly
ignorant of business and such of its perversions as

are called requirements, seemed a mere lamb—a
fancy which was strengthened by the incessant
gesturing and change of position in which he indulged when in conversation. The pair soon separated ; the minister walked away, his step seeming
not so exultant as when he approached the merchant ;
while the latter, appearing to his clerk to be broader,
deeper, and more solid than ever, approached the
store, lifted up his head, displayed the face he
usually wore when he found he had made a bad debt,
and said,

  " George, I wish you wouldn't try to talk about
business to ministers. Old Wedgewell has just
pestered me nearly to death ; says you complain of
having too much to do, and that you have to drink
to keep up. It'll be just like him to tell somebody
else, and a pretty story that'll be to go around about
the chairman of a temperance meeting."

  " I didn't mean to say anything to him," replied
the clerk; " but he made me drop a shutter on my
toes, and I guess that loosened my tongue a little.
I didn't tell him anything but the truth, though,
Squire. I signed the pledge, last night, hoping you'd
help me through."

  " What—what do you mean, George ? " asked

the merchant, in a tone which defined the word
" conservative " more clearly than lexicographer
ever did.

" I can't work so many hours a day without
drinking sometimes," replied the clerk. " What I
ask of you is to take a boy. If I could come in a
couple of hours later every morning—and there's
next to nothing done in the first two hours of the
day—I could have a decent amount of rest, not
have to hurry so much, and wouldn't break down so
often, and have to go to whisky to be helped up
again."

" A boy would have to be paid," remarked ·the
Squire in the tone he habitually used when making
a penitential speech in class-meeting ; " and here's
summer-time coming ; there isn't much business
done in summer, you know."

" A boy won't cost more than a dollar a week the
first year," replied the clerk, " and you'd make that
out of the people who sometimes *have* to go somewhere else and trade on days when you're not here
and I'm too busy to wait on them.   There *isn't* so
much money made in summer ; but women come to
the store then a good deal more than they do in the
winter, and they take up an awful amount of time.

Besides, the store has to be opened about two hours earlier every morning than it does in winter."

The merchant pinched his gloomy brow and reflected. Doughty looked at him without much hopefulness. The Squire's heart might be all right, but his pocket-book was by far the more sensitive and controlling organ. At last the Squire said,

" Well, if it's for *your* good that you want the boy, you ought to be willing to pay his salary. Besides——"

" Excuse me, Squire Temple," interrupted Doughty ; " 'tisn't for my good alone. ' Accursed be he who putteth the bottle to his brother's lips.' I've heard you quote that to more than one man right in this store. That's what you're doing to me if you keep on. You sell half as much again as any other storekeeper in town, and why ? Because I am smart enough to hold custom. I haven't cared to do anything else. I've given myself up to making and holding custom for you, and I took to whisky to keep me up to my work."

" Well, haven't I paid you for all you've done ? " demanded the proprietor.

" Yes ; but now I ask you to pay a little more. I've told you why ; and now the case stands just

here: which do you care for most, the price of a
boy or the soul of your faithful clerk? *You* say a
man's soul's in danger if he drinks."

"Well, I'll tell you, George," replied the Squire,
"I'll think about it. I want to do what's right;
but I—I don't like to have other people's sins fast-
ened on me."

CHAPTER III.

A WET BLANKET.

THE first task to which the penitent Crupp devoted himself on the morning after the meeting was hardly that which his new admirers had supposed he would attempt. They imagined he would knock in the heads of his barrels, and allow the accursed contents to flood his cellar; but Crupp, on the contrary, closed out the entire lot, for cash, at the highest prices he could exact from dealers with whom he had lately been in competition. "'Twas a splendid lot of liquors," said Crupp, in the course of an explanatory speech at the post-office, while every one was waiting for the opening of the regular daily mail; "and though I *do* feel above sellin' 'em over the counter, they're better for men that *will* drink than any that have ever come into Barton since I've been here."

With easier mind and heavier pocket, the ex-rumseller then called upon the Rev. Jonas Wedgewell. That good man's domestic, although from an

ever-green isle whose children do not generally
regard whisky with abhorrence, had sympathetically caught the spirit of her employers, and as she
had not heard of Mr. Crupp's change of mind, she
left him standing on the piazza while she called Mr.
Wedgewell. The divine descended the stairway
two steps at a time, dived into the parlor, and had a
congratulatory speech half delivered before he discovered that the new convert was not there. He
wildly shouted, " Mr. Crupp! " traced the penitent
by his voice, escorted him to the parlor with a series
of hand-shakings, shoulder-pattings, and bows, and
forcibly dropped him into an elegant chair which
Mrs. Wedgewell had bought only to show, and in
which no member of the family had ever dared to sit.

" Ah, my valiant friend," said the Rev. Jonas,
hastily drawing a chair near Mr. Crupp, and shed-
ding upon him the full effulgence of a countenance
beaming with enthusiastic adoration; " the morning
songs of the angels of God must have been sweeter
this morning as they thought of your noble deed.
You have cast off the shackles of a most accursed
bondage. Doubtless you wish to fulfill all of the
conditions of the liberty with which Christ hath
made you free. The church——"

"Excuse me, parson," interrupted Mr. Crupp; "but I don't want to join the church—not just now, anyhow. I——"

"Wish to consecrate your ill-gotten gains to the service of the Lord," broke in the good pastor; but Mr. Crupp frowned, then pouted, then compressed his lips tightly, and gave so sudden a twitch as to wrench one of the joints of the sacred chair, as he replied:

"No, sir, I don't, for I haven't any ill-gotten gains. I never sold anything but good liquor, and the price was always fair. I never sold any liquor to a drunken man, either. What I came to you for is this: I know who drinks, when they drink, what they take, and I know pretty well *why* they drink. Some of them signed the pledge last night, and they're going to have an awful hard job in keeping it."

"Prayer——" interrupted the minister, but the hard-headed Crupp quickly completed the sentence.

"Prayer never cured a dyspeptic stomach, that I've heard of, and I don't believe it'll take away a man's hunger for whisky. These fellows that's been drinking, and have got anything to 'em, *can* be kept from falling into the old ways again; but

they've got to be handled carefully, and what I
came to you for was to ask who was going to do
the handling? You know who's free-handed with
money in your congregation, and free-handed men
ought to be free-hearted. I'm going to Dominie
Brown on the same errand, and to the other
preachers, too."

Mr. Crupp's speech consumed only a moment of
time, but its effect upon the preacher was wonder-
ful—and depressing. From being a mirror of irrepressible Christian exultation, Mr. Wedgewell's face
became as solemn as it ever was when he bemoaned
from the pulpit the apathy of the elect. His eyes
enlarged behind his glasses, and he stared for a
moment in an abstracted manner at a dreadful
chromo which hung upon his wall—a chromo at
which no one in active possession of his mental
faculties could possibly have looked so long. But
the old pastor had a heart so great that even his
theology had been unable to wall it in, and after a
moment of inevitable despondency he realized that
Crupp was intent upon doing good.

"Mr. Crupp," said he, turning his head suddenly,
and regaining a portion of his earlier expression of
countenance, "I do not fully comprehend your in-

tention, but I can see that it is good. May I ask what the people of God can do for these beings who have been under the dominion of alcohol?"

"Well, it's a long story," replied the old bartender. "Among them that signed, there isn't one in ten that ever drank, and of them that drank, half of 'em'll take something before night."

"And break their solemn vow! Awful! awful!" ejaculated the minister.

"Yes," said Crupp, "'*tis* awful; but, on the other hand, there's some that's in earnest. There's Tom Adams, now—he that drives the brick-yard team. Tom's a good, square, honest fellow, and he loves his family, but I don't see how he's going to stop drinking. He can't work without it; leastways, he can't work along the way he's working now. Deacon Jones ought to give him easier work to do until he can bring himself around; but Deacon Jones won't waste his money in that way, if he *is* a member of your church. Then there's old Bunley: there isn't anything *to* him. He's been drinking and drinking and drinking this forty year, he says, and yet he was well brought up, and he can't keep himself from going to church every Sunday. He's got some children that ain't grown yet, and if

some of the storekeepers would only give him credit
without ever expecting to see their money again,
the old fellow wouldn't get down-hearted so often,
and maybe he could quit drinking. As far as taking
care of his family goes, he isn't good for much the
way he is ; he borrows from soft-hearted fellows who
can't afford to lose as well as the storekeepers can,
and *maybe* he steals sometimes—I don't say he
does, mind. At any rate, the biggest part of his
support comes out of the public, and as the public can't help itself, it ought to be sensible enough
to try to make the old chap feel and act like a
man."

"Bless me!" exclaimed Mr. Wedgewell, who had
through all Mr. Crupp's delivery sat erect with his
hands upon his knees, and his eyes and mouth wide
open. "I assure you, my dear sir, that I never had
an idea that the success of the temperance cause
depended upon so many conditions, and I also beg
to assure you"—here the Reverend Jonas hastily
proffered his right hand—"that I appreciate and
admire the spirit which has prompted you to exam-
ine this subject in so many of its bearings, and to
endeavor to throw light upon it. But surely all
the—the men who, as you express it, have been

drinking—surely these cannot be constrained to continue by conditions similar to those which you have instanced? There must be some who, if only they exercise their will-power, will succeed in putting their vile enemy under their feet?"

"Yes," replied Crupp, "there *are* such. Lots of young fellows drink only because they think it's smart, and because they haven't got man enough in them to stop when they want to. They're like a lot of wolves—plucky enough when they're together, but a live rooster could scare one of them if he caught him alone. *I'm* going to look out for *that* crowd myself; they need somebody to preach to 'em wherever he can catch 'em, and I know where they hang out. But I'm not through with the other kind yet. There's Fred Macdonald, he's going to be the hardest man to manage in the whole lot. Good family, you know—got a judge for a father, and ambitious as the——ambitious as Napoleon Bonaparte. He's in with all the steamboat fellows, and whisky is an angel alongside of some things they carry. They'll ruin him, sure. Steamboating looks like something big to him, you know; it shows off better than country stores and saw-mills. It's no use talkin' to him; I've tried it once or twice, for I

know the steamboat people of old ; but he as good
as told me to mind my own business.   Now if some
of the business men could get up something enterprising, and put Fred at the head of it, on condition
that he wouldn't drink any more, they might make
money and save him from going to the—the bad.
I'll put some money into the thing, for I believe in
Fred.   Of course he'll have to be watched a little, for
he may be too venturesome ; but he can get more
trade and get more work out of his men than any
other man in this county."

" Mr. Crupp," said the minister, again taking the
hand of the newly-made reformer, and laying his
own left hand affectionately upon Mr. Crupp's right
elbow, " I cannot find words adequate to the expression of my admiration of your earnestness in
this great moral movement.   But I must confess
that your treatment of the subject is one to which
I am utterly unaccustomed.   I have been wont to
regard intemperance solely as an indication of an in-
firm will and a depraved appetite, but your theory
seems plausible ; indeed, I do not see that either of
our respective standpoints need be wrong.   But,
with regard to the employment of the reformatory
means you suggest, I am not a capable adviser.   It

might be well for you to consult some of our leading business men."

"That's what I am going to do," replied Crupp.
"And I am going to see the doctors, too, and all the
other ministers. What I want of *you* is, to back me
up; preach at these fellows that are well enough off
to make themselves useful."

"I'll do it!" replied the minister with emphasis.
"A suitable text has already providentially entered
my mind: 'Am I my brother's keeper?' Three
heads and application: *First*, demonstrate that every
man *is* his brother's keeper; *second*, show how in
the divine economy it is wise that this should be so;
third, the example of Christ; *application*, our duty
to the needy in our midst. Another text suggests
itself: 'We, then, that are strong ought to bear the
infirmities of the weak.' And yet another: 'Give
strong drink unto him that is ready to perish;'
argument to be that if the Inspired Word justifies
such action as that implied by the text, and if alcohol is the demon we believe it to be, it is our duty
to prevent, by any means in our power, people from
reaching a condition in which such a terrible remedy
must be used. I beg your pardon, my dear Mr.
Crupp," exclaimed the minister, springing excitedly

from his chair; "but if you have any other calls to
make, I will repair at once to my study and pre-
pare a discourse based upon one of these texts.
Excuse my seeming rudeness in thus abruptly
closing our interview, but my soul is on fire—on
fire with ardor which I cannot but believe is from
heaven."

"Oh, certainly," replied Mr. Crupp, rising quite
briskly. "Business is business; it's so in the liquor
trade, I know, and I suppose it is in preaching. I'll
go down and see Squire Tomple, I guess."

The Rev. Jonas Wedgewell dropped abruptly into
a chair, and the fire with which his soul had been
consuming seemed suddenly to expire. His face
became blank and expressionless, his lower jaw
dropped a little, and he gasped,

"Squire Tomple? I had a discouraging conversation with him only yesterday morning on a subject
involving very nearly the ideas which you have advanced. His very estimable clerk, George Doughty,
who signed the pledge at our meeting, asserted that
his work must decrease in volume in order that he
might continue faithful; so I made haste to inter-
cede for him with his employer, but I did not
meet with that encouragement which I had hoped

for. Brother Tomple intimated that temperance
was temperance and business was business, and
even made some remarks which have since seemed
to me to contain implications that I was unduly
concerned about his affairs."

"Tomple's a—a hog, if he *is* a church member,"
replied the irreverent Crupp; "but he's got to make
himself useful if plain talk will do it. It takes all
kinds of men to make a world, parson, or to make
men act like men to their neighbors. Perhaps if
you preachers come down on rich men who hoard
their money, and poor men that are about as stingy
with how-d'ye-do's, and if business men show the
public that it's as cheap to reform a pauper as it is
to support him, and that it isn't the thing to stand
by, while a man's killing himself, without sayin' a
word or spendin' a cent to prevent him—perhaps we
can be of some use in the world. Good day, parson."

2*

CHAPTER IV.

REFORM WITH MONEY IN IT.

TOM ADAMS, driver of the brick-yard wagon, and signer of one of the pledges circulated at the great temperance meeting, was certainly a man worth saving. He had a wife and was rich in children. His wife was faithful, good-natured, and industrious, and his children were of that bright, irrepressible nature which is about the most valuable of inheritances in this land where other inheritances do not average largely in money value. For the good of such a group it was very desirable that the head of the family should be in the constant possession of strong arms and all his wits. And even for his own sake Tom was worth a great deal more attention than men of his kind ever receive. He was perfectly honest, a hard worker, cheerier in temperament than any pastor in the village, quicker-witted than most of the lawyers within the judicial circuit upon which the town of Barton was situated, and more generous in proportion to his means than

any of his well-to-do fellow-citizens. During the
season for making and delivering bricks he worked
from sunrise to sunset, rendered fair count to seller
and buyer, and never abused his employer's horses.
His regular pay was seventy-five cents per day,
which sum, in a land where flour was sold at two
cents per pound and meat was only twice as high as
flour, and a comfortable house could be hired at
four dollars per month, paid his family expenses.
But the season at the brick-yard lasted only during
six months of the twelve.   During the remaining six
months Tom gladly did any work he could find : he
drove teams where any hauling was to be done,
chopped wood, worked in the pork-houses where
merchants prepared for the Southern market the
fatted hogs which were the principal legal-tenders
for the indebtedness of farmer customers, formed part
of the crew of one of the many flatboats which conveyed the meat to market, and did whatever other
work he could find.   But in the winter season, when
the family appetite was most industrious, Tom could
not find employment for all his time, while the
merchants who trusted him made more frequent
requests for money than Tom was able to honor.
When he was idle, he found himself more welcome

at the liquor-shops than anywhere else; when he grew despondent at his inability to pay, he sought solace at these same places; when in the steady work and long hours of the summer season he became gradually "worked out" and "used up"—experiences not infrequent with Tom—he went to the liquor-shops for the only relief he had ever been able to find. His experience did not differ greatly from that of men of higher social standing, who, under similar mental and physical conditions, drink high-priced wines. He gradually increased the quantity of his potations, and went through the successive experiences of being unmanned by liquor, striving to rebuild himself by the power which had broken him, becoming by turns gay, silly, boisterous, pugnacious, sullen, apathetic, and finally penitent. Each of his sprees cost him several days in time and several dollars in money—a fact which no one realized more clearly than Tom himself; yet the feeling which had made him take the first drinks of these frightful series was one which had its seat in his own better nature, and which he had many times found more powerful than every influence he could bring to bear against it. He had listened to many a private lecture on the subject of his weakness, and had honestly admitted the truth of all that was said to him on the subject; he had signed many a pledge in the most agonized earnest, and had broken every one of them.

On the Monday which followed the temperance meeting Tom Adams was nearly frantic with his old longing. The rest of Sunday had been a hindrance rather than a help to him, for he had already suffered several days from the effects of abstaining from his usual after-dinner and after-supper potations. The amount usually drank on these occasions had not been great, but the habit had for some years been so regular that his amazed and indignant physique protested against the change. Had he been capable of spiritually withdrawing himself from the world on the day of the Lord, he might have found help and strength; but he was as incapable of such a thing as were nine-tenths of the church-members in Barton. While he remained at home, his children were noisy enough to have hurried a rapt seer back to the realization of earthly things; when he went abroad he could not, as was his usual Sunday habit, step quietly into the back door of Bayne's liquor-store. He strolled down to the stable-yard of the Barton House, hoping to find some one with whom he could talk horse; but the hostler was not in sight, and the stable-boy, who had been heard to say he " didn't count much on them fellers what signed the pledge and went back on their friends," eyed him with evident disgust. In the street he met people going to and from church and Sunday-school, and they looked at him as if their eyes were asking, " Are you keeping your pledge?" Then, to crown all, his wife gave him such a beseeching and yet doubting look every time he left the house and returned to it that he almost hated the good woman for her affectionate anxiety.

Tom was up bright and early Monday morning, and though he soon mounted his wagon and left his wife's eyes behind him, he found his longing for liquor as close to him as ever. Reaching the brick-yard, he was rather startled to find there Deacon Jones, his employer, and owner of a store as well as the kilns. The deacon looked at him as all the religious people had done on Sunday, and Tom inwardly cursed him.

" How are you, Tom?" inquired the deacon, and then, without waiting for a reply, remarked:

" There's somethin' I've been a-wantin' to talk to you 'bout, Tom, an' I was sure o' catchin' you here, so I came over before breakfast. You signed the pledge t'other night."

This latter clause was delivered with an accompanying glance which caused Tom to put a great deal of anger into his reply, although his words were few.

"Yes, an' kep' it, too."

"I'm glad of it, Tom. There's been times when you didn't, you know. Well, what I want to say is this: Some folks say that some men drink because they have to work too hard, an' because they have trouble. Now, mebbe—I only say mebbe, mind—*mebbe* that's what upset you those other times. Now, if I was to give you work all the year round at seventy-five cents a day, an' not work you more'n ten hours a day, would it help you to keep straight?"

"Would it?" said Tom, scratching his head, wrinkling his brows, and eying the deacon incredulously "Why, of course it would."

"Well, then," said the deacon, "I'll do it. As long as the brick business is good you can work at haulin' from seven to twelve, an' one to six. Don't you s'pose you could put two or three hundred more brick on a load without hurtin' the hosses? I don't want to lose any more'n I can help, you know, by cuttin' down your time. Rainy days I'll keep you busy at the store some way; them's the days farm- ers can't do much on the farm, so they bring their butter and eggs to town, and there's a sight of meas- urin' an' weighin' to be done. An' after the brick season's over I'll find you somethin' to do at the store. You can put the pork-house an' warehouse to rights before the packin' season begins, an' you can weigh the corn an' wheat an' oats an' pork when they come in, and mend bags, and work in the pork-house three months out of the six. You wouldn't object to takin' night-spells in the pork- house instead of day-spells, would you, when we have to work day *and* night? Night-wages costs us most, you know, an' you ought to help us make up what we lose on you when there's nothin' doin'."

" Just as *you* say," replied Tom. He did not clasp the deacon in a grateful embrace, for the deacon had, in his thrifty way, prevented Tom from feeling es- pecially grateful. The owner of the brick-yard had intimated that the new arrangement was for Tom's especial benefit, but his later remarks caused this feature of the arrangement to speedily disappear from view. But, although not doubting for an instant that the deacon meant to get his money back with usury, Tom felt his heart growing lighter every moment. At the same time he felt angry at the deacon's occasional suggestions that the arrangements were partly of the nature of charity. So he replied:

"Just as *you* say; but, deacon, I ain't the feller that wants money for work I don't do, *you* know that. The arrangement suits me first-rate, but I'm goin' to work hard for my money; you can bet all your loose change on *that*."

"Thomas!" ejaculated the deacon sternly, "I am not in the habit of betting. It's a careless, foolish, wasteful, sinful way of using money."

"That's so," replied Tom reflectively; "unless," he continued, "you're one of the winnin' kind."

"It is a business I don't intend to go into, so the less said of it the better. So my offer suits you, does it?"

"I'll shake hands on it," replied Tom, extending his hand.

"Wait a moment," said the deacon, retiring his own right hand to a conservative position behind his back. "If it suits you," continued the deacon impressively, "you agree to stick to your pledge; no foolin' with whisky again, mind."

"Nary drop," said Tom, with great emphasis. "Ten minutes ago I wouldn't have given a pewter dime for my chance of sticking it out through the day, but now I wouldn't give a cent for a barr'l full of ten-year-old rye."

"All right, then—shake hands. And we begin to-day—or say to-morrow—there's lots of bricks wanted to-day—here's the orders. And may the Lord help you, Thomas—help you to hold out steadfast unto the end. Now I reckon I'll get home to breakfast."

As the deacon walked off he soliloquized in this manner:

"There! I wonder if that'll suit Crupp an' Brother Wedgewell? What a queer team them two fellows make! Queer that Crupp should have bothered me two hours Saturday night, an' the preacher should have come out so strong about bein' our brothers' keepers the very next day. 'Twas a Christian act for me to do, too. 'He that converteth a sinner from the error of his ways'— ah! blessed be the promises. An' I won't lose a cent by the operation—*I* can keep him busy enough. When folks know what I've done an' what I done it for, I guess they'll think I've got my good streaks after all. I declare, I ought to have told him I couldn't pay for days when he was sick; 'tain't too late yet, though—he won't back out on *that* account. Mebbe I can talk him into j'ining the church, too—who knows, an' some day in 'xperience meetin' mebbe he'll tell how it all came about through me. He must bring his dinners with him when he's workin' about the store. I ought to have done that with my clerk before he took to lunchin' off the crackers and cheese busy days—these little things all cost. But it *does* make a man feel good to do kindnesses to his fellow-men."

As for Tom Adams, he mounted the wagon, seized the reins, and exclaimed,

" By thunder! 'fore I haul a durned brick, I'll just drive home by the back way and tell the old woman. Reckon she won't look at me any more in *that* way then. Like enough he's right when he says *some* says mebbe workin' too hard makes fellows drink. It never got into *my* head before, though."

As Tom drove through a back street in which Mr. Crupp lived, that worthy stared at the empty wagon inquiringly.

"The old man's engaged me for a year, at six bits a day, and only ten hours a day to work," shouted Tom in explanation.

"The devil!" replied the new reformer, and seizing his hat he hurried off to the Rev. Jonas Wedgewell. The pastor was discovered through an open window at his matutinal repast, and the eager Crupp thrust his head in the window and shouted,

"First blood, parson! Old Jones has hired Tom for a year, and he's only got ten hours a day to work."

The holy man raised his hands, despite the incumbrances of half a biscuit and a coffee cup, and exclaimed,

"Bless the Lord for the first fruits of the seed so newly sown. Who would have thought so undemonstrative a man would have been the first to heed the word of exhortation?"

"He's the first to see money in it—that's why," explained Crupp.

"My dear sir, do you really ascribe Deacon Jones's

meritorious action to sordid motives?" asked the old pastor, opening his mouth and eyes as if the answer for which he waited was to come through them.

"Hum—well, no—I reckon 'twas a little mixed," replied Mr. Crupp, meditatively analyzing a blossom of a honeysuckle growing by the pastor's window. "I dinged at him, you preached at him, he thought it over, and whatever Jonathan Jones thinks over long is pretty sure to have money in it somewhere in the end. He'll make mor'n he'll lose on Tom, an' it's best he should—he'll have a better heart to try another experiment of the same sort one of these days. But I didn't mean to interrupt your breakfast—beg your pardon, Mrs. Wedgewell and young ladies, for not ringing the bell, but I was too full of the news to behave myself. Good by."

And Mr. Crupp started for his own breakfast-table, while the Reverend Jonas's eyes seemed directed at some object just out of sight, as he abstractedly raised his coffee cup to his lips.

CHAPTER V.

WHY old Bunley had made Barton his place of residence nobody knew. The most plausible theory ever advanced on the subject came from the former proprietor of the Barton House, who said that Bunley, happening to be traveling that way, had found the brandy at the Barton House so good that he hadn't the heart to leave it. The brandy lasted so long that old Bunley—then twenty years younger—while consuming it became acquainted with nearly everybody in the town; and as he had no engagements that restrained him from making himself agreeable, he found himself well liked, and entreated to make his home at Barton. He reported—and his report was afterward verified —that he was the son of a Virginia planter, and was unpopular at home because he had made a runaway match with a splendid girl, whose only fault was that her family did not rank very high. Bunley's father had cut his son off with a thousand dollars,

but had considerately sent the money with the letter of dismissal; so the happy couple were leisurely
spending the money and waiting for the old gentleman to relent, as irate fathers always do in books.
But while Bunley was enjoying the hospitalities of
Barton, annoyed only by the fact that his purse was
growing light, he heard of his father's sudden death
and of the inheritance by an unloving brother of the
entire estate. Then the young bridegroom attempted to obtain money by borrowing, for this was the
only method of money-getting he understood; but
the small success which attended his efforts did not
pay for the annoyance which his soulless creditors
gave him. Then he tried gambling, and, by devot-
ing his mind to it, succeeded so well that no one
but an occasional commercial traveler, to whom
Bunley's ways were unknown, would play with him.
Then, under the guise of being clerk of the Barton
House, he became its actual barkeeper, and attracted so much custom away from the other liquor-
sellers that the grateful proprietor took him into
partnership, and, dying a year later, bequeathed the
whole business to him. But the good brandy which
had first persuaded Bunley to stop at Barton continued its fascinations, and the new proprietor of

the Barton House, while liked by all travelers, grew so unpopular with purveyors of flour, meat, and other hotel necessities that the sheriff was finally called upon to settle the differences between them by disposing of the hotel property at auction.

After that Bunley ran to seed, to use an expression common in Barton. How he lived during the twenty years which followed was not well understood. His wife died, and it was understood that he married some money the second time; but it was none the less whispered about town that Bunley had been seen at night to borrow at woodpiles whose owners he had not consulted. He went upon mighty sprees, and carried the bouquet of liquor wherever he went. He started a small groggery of his own, in which many bright boys learned to drink. He had long since ruined the credit which he obtained on the strength of his second wife's property, for he never paid an account.

And yet the most aggrieved of Bunley's creditors could not help being soft-hearted when they saw the old man in church, as he was every Sunday morning with his two boys. The gentleman which was in old Bunley then showed itself in his face and manner, and it *did* seem too bad that any one who

could look and act so much like a man should not
be trusted to the extent of a dollar's worth of sugar
or a hundred pounds of flour. Squire Tomple had
thought so one Sunday, and as the Squire strove to
keep worldly thoughts out of his mind on the Lord's
day, his mind became filled with old Bunley—so
much so, that on the following Monday he decoyed
Bunley into his store, and talked so pleasantly to
him that the old gentleman actually made the
request for which the Squire hoped. He bought
rather more than the Squire had meant to sell him
on credit, but his promise of early payment was so
distinct and emphatic that the Squire's doubt was
not fairly established for many months. This story
in all its details was told by the Squire to Mr.
Crupp, after that gentleman announced to him that
something should be done for old Bunley.

" That was because you didn't go about the job in
the right way," said Crupp. " He's got just enough
conceit to suppose that he's going to pay all his
bills some day, and he feels that when the time
comes your profit'll pay for your kindness. That
conceit of his is just what needs to be taken down
—it's got to be done kindly—so that he under-
stands that whatever he gets comes out of pure

3

charity and the desire to make him comfortable, even at a loss. Now, he and his little family can live on about a dollar a day. I'll stand half the expense of supporting him for three months if you'll do the other half, and we'll talk plain, good-natured English to him, and let him understand he's a pauper. That'll put him on his mettle. What do you say?"

The Squire looked grave at once—as grave as he had appeared when an uninsured hogshead of sugar belonging to him had fallen from a steamboat gangplank into the river, and melted. The proposition seemed to take his breath away, in fact; but in a moment or two he regained it.

"Look here, Crupp," said he, "temperance is all very well; but I don't think it's my business to stand part of the expenses of reforming everybody, when I haven't had anything to do with making drunkards. With you the case is different. You say your liquors were always good; but, like enough, that made men all the fonder of drinking the infernal things. You're a public-spirited citizen, but you can't deny that you've had a thousand times more to do with making drunkards than I have. The very fact that you *are* a decent fellow yourself has made drinking halfway respectable in Barton. The crime's right at your own door, and you ought to pay for it. You——"

The Squire paused. Mr. Crupp's face was very white and his teeth were tightly set. Mr. Crupp *had* been known to throw a disorderly visitor at his bar halfway across the street; and although the Squire knew that his own avoirdupois was too great to be treated so contemptuously, he had no desire to feel the weight of Crupp's fist. Besides, Crupp was a customer who bought a great deal and paid promptly, and the Squire did not like to offend him and lose his custom. So the Squire paused.

"Go right on," said Mr. Crupp very quietly. "I'll not bear any malice. I've said a great many worse things to myself. Don't hold in anything you've got on your mind."

"I'm done," said the Squire, looking relieved and extending his hand. "Crupp, I think a good deal of you, and I'm ashamed of myself for boiling over as I did. But folks talk to me as if I was made of money. I paid out a good deal on the expense of the meeting; the parson's been at me to help every lazy drunkard to get work; George Doughty wants more pay or less work, so he won't have such a hankering after liquor; and now to be asked to help old Bunley, that's owed me money a long time and never paid it, that came near helping one of my boys to a taste for liquor, that helps himself at my woodpile—it's *too* much, that's all."

"Squire," said Crupp, "isn't there something in your Bible that's not complimentary to men who say to the needy, 'Depart: be ye warmed and fed,' but don't put their hands into their pockets to help the poor wretches along? I tell you that a man that's got the love of drink fixed in every muscle in his body and every drop of his blood is worse off than any cold and hungry man you ever saw. Such men *sometimes* help themselves out of their trouble, and stick to cold water; but the man that does it is more of a hero, and he's got better stuff in him, than any other sort of sinner that ever repents. He's got to be helped just like drowning men have to be, and you've got to take hold of him just as you do of a drowning man, by whatever part you can get the tightest grip on. Bunley's pride's the only handle you can find on *him*, and you can't get at *that* except by showing that you think enough of him to sink money in him."

The Squire cast about in his mind for some argu-

ment in defense of his money; but, as he found none,
he acted like a good diplomatist, and started to talk
against time by uttering some promising generali-
zations.

"I always meant, and I still mean," said he, "to
do good with my money. That's what it was given
me for. I'm only the Lord's steward——"

"And right here in Barton is where the Lord put
you to do it," said Crupp. "Here's where you
made your money; here are the people who know
you and don't suspect you of caring any less for
your money than other folks do for theirs; here
are the people you know all about; you know their
weaknesses and their good points, and every dollar
you spend on them you can watch, and see that it
does its duty."

"When I *know* that helping a man will be sure to
reform him," began the Squire, when again his com
panion interrupted him:

"Did you ever read of Christ's letting a man suffer for fear that if he cured him or fed him he
might get sick or hungry again? If I read straight,
he helped everybody that came to him, and everybody that needed help. I suppose loafers were as
thick in Judæa as they are in Barton; why, when he

healed those ten lepers there was only one of them decent enough to come back and say " Thank you." *I've* got money enough to take Bunley on my own shoulders for a little while, and I'm going to spend a good deal on such fellows; but they want to see that they're thought something of by men who never sold whisky, who never made anything out of them, who are enough in earnest to do something for them that costs more than talk does. I know it isn't easy, but it's got to be done—that is, if Christianity is true."

Crupp's last shot told. Squire Tomple was orthodox, but he was not without reflective capacity, and many had been his twinges of conscience at his practical rejection of undoubted deductions which he had drawn from Christ's teachings and example. But on this particular occasion, as on many others, he was not defeated ; he was only temporarily demoralized. In a moment he was on the defensive again, and suddenly raised his head and opened his lips ; but, whatever his idea was, it remained unspoken; for in the eye of Crupp, which had been intently scrutinizing his face and through it his heart, he detected a softness and haziness unusual in the eyes of men. The Squire, not without a struggle, became at once shamefaced and obedient, and said hurriedly,

"Crupp, you're a good, square man; I'm proud to know you, and I'll do what you like—for old Bunley, that is."

Great was the surprise of Bunley himself, when he answered a knock at his door a few minutes later, to find Squire Tomple and Mr. Crupp upon his front stoop, both of them looking and acting as if extremely embarrassed. But old Bunley never forgot his Virginia breeding, not even before a couple of creditors; so he invited both gentlemen to seats on the top step, and then sat down between them.

The Squire looked appealingly at Crupp; Crupp winked encouragingly at the Squire; the Squire coughed feebly; Crupp plucked a stem of timothy grass, and gazed at it as if he had never seen such a thing before; the Squire took out a pocket-knife, and began to scrape his finger-nails, and then Crupp remarked that it was a fine day. Bunley having cheerfully assented to this expression of opinion, there was a moment or two of awkward silence, which was finally relieved by Bunley, who drew from his pocket a plug of tobacco, from which he took a bite, after first offering it to his visitors. A little more facial pantomime went on between Tomple and Crupp, and then the Squire spoke.

" Bunley," said he, " you don't seem to get along very fast in the world."

" That's a fact," answered Bunley with hearty emphasis. " Luck seems to go against me, no matter how I lay myself out. There ain't a man in this town that wants to do the right thing any more than I do, but somehow I don't get' the chance. I signed the pledge t'other night at the meetin'; but how I'm goin' to stick to it, with all the trouble I'm in, is more than I can see through."

" We've come down to help you do it," said the Squire.

" To help you with money—not talk," supplemented Crupp.

Bunley looked at both men quickly, from under the extreme inner edge of his upper eyelid.

" We propose, between us, to show you that we're in dead earnest to help you keep the pledge," continued the Squire. " We're going to give you, week after week, whatever you need to live on for the next three months, so you won't have any excuse for drinking to drown trouble, and so you'll have a chance to find something to do."

Old Bunley sprang to his feet. "Gentlemen,"
said he, "you're—you're *gentlemen.* It's the first
time in my life that anybody ever cared *that* much
for me, though. You shan't lose anything by it, I
promise you *that;* I'll pay you back again the first
chance I get to make anything."

"We don't *want* it back," said Crupp. "We
won't *take* it back. We want to *give* it to you, out
and out——"

"To show you that it's *you* that we're interested
in, not ourselves," interrupted the Squire.

Then Old Virginia came to the surface again;
Bunley seemed to grow an inch or two, and to swell
several more as he replied,

"I'm not a pauper, gentlemen."

"Certainly not," said the Squire hastily; "but you
can't pay your debts nor your current expenses,
and Crupp and I are a little ahead in the world, and
willing to give you a hundred, say—a little at a
time."

"You've got a couple of boys to bring up, you
know, Bunley," suggested Crupp.

"And they ought to go among the best people,
too," said the Squire. "You came of a good family——"

3*

"And their mother was a lady, too—every inch of her!" exclaimed Bunley.

"Of course she was," said Crupp. "But, to come back to business, we don't want you to have any excuse to touch whisky again, and we want you to live on us for the next three months as a personal favor. After that, if you make any money, I s'pose the Squire'll be glad to sell you anything he keeps in his store; I know *I* will, if I'm in business then. But you mustn't talk about paying now, 'cause it's all nonsense. Come up to the Squire's store when you want anything. Good-by."

Bunley drew himself up with great solemnity and old-time courtesy as he shook hands with both men. When his visitors reached the friendly angle of an old, abandoned barn, both turned hastily, gazed through cracks between the boards, and saw the old man sitting in a meditative attitude, with his lower jaw in both his hands.

"*Don't* that look good?" whispered Crupp, his face all animation.

"It does that," replied the Squire; "there's no dodging the question; it *does* look good."

CHAPTER VI.

A COURSE NEVER SMOOTH.

ON a pleasant August evening, at that particular portion of the day in which twilight shades into night, Fred Macdonald left his father's house and walked toward the opposite portion of the village. From his leisurely, elastic gait, the artistic effect of his necktie, the pose of his hat, the rosebud in his button-hole, and the graceful carriage of his cane, it was very evident that Frederick's steps did not tend toward the fulfillment of any prosaic business engagement. It was not so dark that he could not recognize, in occasional unlighted windows, certain faces well known, some of them handsome, all of them pleasing ; nor was it too dark, just after Fred had bestowed a bow and a smile upon the occupant of each of these windows, and passed on, for one to discern, by the expressions upon most of the faces that slowly turned and looked after the young man, that Fred need not have gone farther in search of a cordial welcome. But he walked on

until he reached the residence of the Rev. Jonas
Wedgewell. To any one not a resident of Barton
the house might have seemed a strange one to be
visited by a young man fond of liquor and the company frequently found on Western steamboats ; and
the stranger's surprise might have increased, at finding that Fred had been so frequent a visitor that
even the house itself seemed glad to see him, and
that the heavy old door seemingly opened of its
own accord, before Fred's fingers had time to touch
its antique knocker. But had the supposititious
observer possessed good eyes, whose actual powers
were temporarily increased by the stimulus of curiosity, his bewilderment would have ended a second
later ; for, as Fred stepped inside the hall, there came
from behind the door a small hand, and then a
dainty ruffle, and then a muslin sleeve, and these all
took their direction toward the shoulder of Fred's
coat ; while there followed a profile which the be-
holder would have willingly gazed upon longer, had
it not almost instantaneously disappeared behind
that side of Fred's face which was farthest from the
door.

Could the observer's gaze have penetrated the
window shades of Parson Wedgewell's little parlor,

he would have seen a face, not girlish or of regular
features, and yet so full of happiness that its effect
was that of absolute beauty and the innocence of
youth. There were estimable maidens in Barton
who, scorning the thought that they could be either
jealous or envious, had frequently remarked to their
intimates that they could *not* see what men found
in Esther Wedgewell to rave about, and it was well
known that the mystery had never been satisfacto-
rily explained to such young ladies as had become
the wives of men who had been among Miss Esther's admirers. It is even to be doubted whether
Fred Macdonald himself could have verbally eluci-
dated the matter; there *have* been such cases where
long and joyous lifetimes have not sufficed in which
to frame such an explanation, and when the person
most blessed has had to journey into another world
in search of adequate power of expression. Ordinarily Esther Wedgewell was a young lady the
pleasantness of whose face did not hide the fact
that its owner's forehead was too high, the nose too
short, the mouth too large, and the complexion too
pale for perfect beauty. But somehow young men
noticed first of all Miss Esther's eyes, and these,
though neither of heavenly blue, nor violet, nor the

brownness of nuts, nor large, nor melting, but only
plain gray, were so honest in themselves, and so
sympathetic for others, that no one of any character cared to gaze from them to any other of the
young woman's features.

What Fred and Esther said to each other during
the first few minutes after their meeting, was of a
nature which never shows to full advantage in print;
besides, it was in the nature of things that they
should say very little.   In spite of the experience
accumulated during a hundred or more of just such
meetings, it seemed necessary that a few minutes
should be consumed by Fred in assuring himself
that it was really Esther who sat in the rocking-
chair in front of him ; and the same time was used
by the lady in determining that the handsome, in-
telligent face in front of her was that of the only
lover she had ever accepted.   Gradually, however,
the sentences spoken by the couple became longer
and more frequent ; their subjects were ordinary
enough ; being the mutual acquaintances they had
met during the day ; the additions which had been
made to the embroidery on the pair of slippers
which Esther, after the manner of most other be-
trothed maidens in America, had begun to make for

her lover; the quality of the singing in church on the preceding Sunday; the latest news from Captain Hall's expedition to the North Pole; the character of Shakespeare's Portia; and yet one would have supposed, from the countenances of both of these young people, that in each of these topics there was some underlying motive of the most delightful import; while their remarks seemed to indicate that there was but one side to either of the subjects discussed, and that both Fred and Esther saw it with the extreme clearness of earthly comprehension.

Then, in a lull in the conversation, Fred asked, with a courtesy and minuteness inherited from aristocratic parents, about Mr. and Mrs. Wedgewell, and elicited the information that Esther's father was composing a second sermon on intemperance.

"Your father undoubtedly is himself the best judge of the needs of his congregation," said Fred, dropping his eyes a little and playing with a bit of paper; "but I can't help feeling that he is wasting his fine talents in preaching on intemperance. If his sermons could be heard and applied by the proper persons, they might do a great deal of good; but what drunkard goes to church? Only moderate drinkers and people who don't drink at all ever hear your father's sermons, and none of them have any need for such instructions."

Esther brushed an imaginary thread or mote from her dress, and said, with some embarrassment,

"Father believes that the moderate drinkers are those who most need to be warned."

"Why, Ettie!" exclaimed Fred, "how can he believe that? He must know that I occasionally—that is, he knows that I am not one of the Sons of Temperance; yet he gave me you"—here conversation ceased a moment as Fred stepped toward Esther, conveying unto that lady an affectionate testimonial whose exact nature will be understood—"and he certainly would not have done so had he supposed I was in any danger of being injured by liquor."

Esther did not wait even until she had finished rearranging a disordered tress or two to reply.

"He said 'yes,' only after I told him of your promise to me that you would not drink any more after we were married. He said you were the best born and best bred young man he had ever met—as if I didn't already know it, you dear boy—but that he

would rather bury me than let me marry a drinking
man."

During the delivery of this short speech Fred
looked by turns astonished, sober, flattered, sullen,
indignant, and finally business-like and judicial.
Then he said :

"Darling, you must let me believe that your father
is not fully posted about men who take an occasional
glass. It's no fault of his ; he probably never tasted
a drop of liquor in his life—he may never have felt
the need of it. But believe me when I tell you that
many of the smartest men drink sometimes, and are
greatly helped by it. A business man whose daily
life can't help being often irregular, sometimes finds
he can't get along without something to help him
through the day. Why, a few days ago I helped
Sam Crayme, captain of the " Excellence," you
know, at a difficult bit of business ; I worked thirty-
six hours on a stretch, and made fifty dollars by it.
That's more money than any of your young temperance men of Barton ever make in a month, but I
never could have done it if it hadn't been for an
occasional drink."

"But," said Esther, "you know I don't say it by
way of complaint, Fred dear, but for a week after

that you felt dull and didn't say much, and didn't care to read, and one evening when I expected you you didn't come."

"But think how tired a man must be after such a job, Ettie," pleaded Fred in an injured tone.

"You poor old fellow, I know it," said Esther; "but you wouldn't have been so if you hadn't done the work, and you yourself say you couldn't have done the work if you hadn't drunk the liquor, and you know you didn't need the money so badly as to have had to do so much. Any merchant in the town would be glad to give you employment at which you would be your own natural self."

"And I would always be a poor man if I worked for our plodding, small-paying merchants," said Fred. "Why, Ettie, who own the handsomest houses in town, who have the best horses, who set the best tables, whose wives and children wear the best clothes? Why, Moshier and Brown and Crayme and Wainwright, every one of them moderate drinkers; I never in my life saw one of them drunk."

"And I would rather be dead than be the wife of any one of them," said Esther with an energy which startled Fred. "Mrs. Moshier used to be such a happy-looking woman, and now she is *so* quiet and has such sad eyes. Brown seems to spend no end of money on his family; but his children are always put to bed before he comes home, because he is as likely as not to be cross and unkind to them; when they meet him on the street they never shout 'Papa!' and rush up to him as your little brothers and sisters do to *your* father; but they look at him first with an anxious look that's enough to break one's heart, and as likely as not cross the street to avoid meeting him. Mrs. Crayme was having *such* a pleasant time at Nellie Wainwright's party the other night, when her husband, who she seldom enough has a chance to take into society with her, said such silly things and stared around with such an odd look in his eye that she made some excuse to take him home. And Nellie Wainwright—she was my particular friend before she was married, you know—was here a few days ago, and I was telling her how happy I was, when suddenly she threw both arms around my neck and burst out crying, and told me that she hoped that my husband would never drink after I was married. She insists upon it that her husband is the best man that ever lived, and that if she only mentions anything she would like, she has it at once if money can buy it, and yet she is unhappy. She says there's always a load on her heart, and though she feels real wicked about it, she can't get rid of it."

Fred Macdonald was unable for some moments to reply to this unexpected speech; he arose from his chair, and walked slowly up and down the room, with his hands behind him, and with the countenance natural to a man who has heard something of which he had previously possessed no idea. Esther looked at him, first furtively, then tenderly; then she sprang to his side and leaned upon his shoulder, saying,

"Dear Fred, I know *you* could never be that way; but then all these women were sure they knew just the same about their lovers, before they were married."

"Well, Ettie," said Fred, passing an arm about the young lady, "I really don't know what's to be done about it, if drinking moderately is the cause of all these dreadful things; I'm bound to *be* somebody; I'm in the set of men that make money; they like me, and I understand them. But they all take something, and you don't know how they look at a man who refuses to drink with them; all of them think he don't amount to much, and some of them actually feel insulted. What is a fellow to do?"

"Go into some other set, I suppose," said Esther very soberly.

"You don't know what you're saying, my dear girl," said Fred. "What else is there for a man to do in a dead-and-alive place like Barton? you don't want to be the wife of a four-hundred-dollar clerk, and live in part of a common little house, do you?"

"Yes," said Esther, showing her lover a rapturous face whose attractiveness was not marred by a suspicion of shyness. "I do, if Fred Macdonald is to be my husband."

"Then if either of us should have a long illness, or if I should lose my position, we would have to depend on your parents and mine," said Fred.

"Let us wait, then," said Esther, "until you can have saved something, before we are married."

"And be like Charley Merrick and Kate Armstrong, who've been engaged for ten years, and are growing old and doleful about it."

"*I'll* never grow old and doleful while waiting for *my* lover to succeed," said Esther, in a tone which might have carried conviction with it had Fred been entirely in a listening humor. But as Fred

imagined himself in the position of the many unsuccessful young men in Barton, and of the anx-
ious-looking husbands who had once been as
spirited as himself, he fell into a frame of mind
which was anything but receptive. In his day-
dreams marriage had seemed made up of many
things beside the perpetual companionship of
Esther : it had among its very desirable compo-
nents a handsome, well-furnished house, a carriage
of the most approved style, an elegant wardrobe
for Esther, and one of faultless style for himself, a
prominent pew in church, and, not least of all, a
sideboard which should be better stocked than that
of any of his friends. To banish these from his
mind for a moment, and imagine himself living in
two or three rooms ; cheapening meat at the butch-
er's ; never driving out but when he could borrow
somebody's horse and antiquated buggy ; wearing
a suit of clothes for two or three years in succession, while Esther should spend hours in making
over and over the dresses of her unmarried days ;
all this made him almost deaf to Esther's loyal
words, and nearly oblivious to the fact that the
wisest and sweetest girl in Barton was resting
within his arm. Suddenly he aroused himself from

his revery, and exclaimed, in a tone which Esther did not at first recognize as his own,

"Ettie, your ideas are honest and lofty, but you must admit that I know best about matters of business. I can't deliberately throw away everything I have done, and form entirely different business connections. I've always regretted my promise to stop drinking after our marriage; but I've trusted that you, with your unusual sense, would see the propriety of absolving me from it."

Esther shrank away from Fred, and hid her face in her hands, whispering hoarsely,

"I can't, I can't, and I never will."

She dropped into a chair and burst into tears. Fred's momentary expression of anger softened into sorrow, but his business instinct did not desert him. "Ettie," said he tenderly, "I thought you trusted me."

"You *know* I do, Fred," said the weeping girl; "but my lover and the Fred who drinks are two different persons, and I *can't* trust the latter. Don't think me selfish: be always your natural self, and there's no poverty or sorrow that I won't endure to be always with you. Do you think I hope to marry you for the sake of living in luxury, or that any

pleasures that money will buy will satisfy me any
more than they do Nellie Wainwright and Mr.
Moshier's wife?   Or do you, professing to love me,
ask me to run even the slightest risk of ever being
as unhappy as the poor women we have been
talking about are with their husbands, who love
them dearly? You *must* keep that promise, or I
must love you apart from you—until you marry
some one else! Even then I could only stop, it
seems to me, by stopping to live."

Fred's face, while Esther was speaking, was anything but comely to look upon, but his intended
reply was prevented by a violent knock at the
door. Esther hurriedly dried her eyes, and prepared to vanish, if necessary, while Fred regained
in haste his ordinary countenance ; then, as the
servant opened the door, the lovers heard a voice
saying,

" Is Fred Macdonald here ? He must come
down to George Doughty's right away. George is
dying ! "

Fred gave Ettie a hasty kiss and a conciliatory
caress, after which he left the house at a lively
run.

CHAPTER VII.

SOME NATURAL RESULTS.

GEORGE DOUGHTY lay propped up in bed;
standing beside him, and clasping his hand
tightly, was his wife; near him were his two oldest
children, seemingly as ignorant of what was transpir-
ing as they were uncomfortable on account of the
peculiar influence which pervaded the room. On the
other side of the bed, and holding one of the dying
man's hands, knelt Parson Wedgewell; beside him
stood the doctor; while behind them both, near the
door, and as nearly invisible as a man of his size could
be, was Squire Tomple. The Squire's face and figure
seemed embodiments of a trembling, abject apology;
he occasionally looked toward the door, as if to
question that inanimate object whether behind its
broad front he, the Squire, might not be safe from
his own fears. It was very evident that the Squire's
conscience was making a coward of him; but it was
also evident, and not for the first time in the world's
history, that cowardice is mightily influential in

4

holding a coward to the ground that he hates. Had
any one spoken to him, or paid him the slightest attention, the Squire would have felt better; nothing
turns cowards into soldiers so quickly as the receipt
of a volley; but no such relief seemed at all likely
to reach him. The doctor, like a true man, having
done all things, could only stand, and stand he did;
Parson Wedgewell, feeling that upon his own efforts
with the Great Physician depended the sick man's
future well-being, prayed silently and earnestly, raising his head only to search, through his tears, the
face of the patient for signs of the desired answer
to prayer. Mrs. Doughty was interested only in
looking into the eyes too soon to close forever, and
the faces of the two children were more than a man
could intentionally look upon a second time. So
when Doughty's baby, who had been creeping about
the floor, suddenly beholding the glories of the great
seal which depended from the Squire's fob-chain,
tried to climb the leg of the storekeeper's trousers,
the Squire smiled, as a saint in extremity might
smile at the sudden appearance of an angel, and he
stooped—no easy operation for a man of Squire
Tomple's bulk—and, lifting the little fellow in his
arms, put kisses all over the tiny face, which, in view

of the relations of cleanliness to attractiveness, was not especially bewitching. A moment later, however, a muffled but approaching step brought back to the Squire his own sense of propriety, and he dropped the baby just in time to be able to give a hand to Fred Macdonald, as that young man softly pushed open the door. The Squire's face again became apologetic.

"How did it happen?" whispered Fred.

"Why," replied the Squire, "the doctor says it's a galloping consumption; *I* never knew a thing about it. Doctor says it's the quickest case he ever knew; he never imagined anything was the matter with George. If *I* d known anything about it, I'd have had the doctor attending him long ago; but George isn't of the complaining kind. The idea of a fellow being at work for me, and dying right straight along. Why, it's awful! He says he never knew anything about it himself, so I don't see how *I* could He was at the store up to four or five days ago then his wife came around one morning and told me that he didn't feel fit to work that day, but she didn't say what the matter was. I've been thinking, for two or three weeks, about giving him some help in the store ; but you know how business drives everything out of a man's head. First I thought I'd stay around the store myself evenings, and let George rest; but I've had to go to lodge meetings and prayer meetings, and my wife's wanted me to go out with her, and so my time's been taken up. Then I thought I'd get a boy, and—well, I didn't know exactly which to do; but if I'd known——"

"But can't something be done to brace him up for a day or two?" interrupted Fred; "then I'll take him out driving every day, and perhaps he'll pick up."

The Squire looked twenty years older for a moment or two as he replied,

"The doctor says he hasn't any physique to rally upon; he's all gone, muscle, blood, and everything. It's the queerest thing I ever knew; he hasn't had anything to do, these past few years, but just what *I* did when I was a young man."

The dying man turned his eyes inquiringly, and asked in a very thin voice,

"Isn't Fred here?"

Fred started from the Squire's side, but the storekeeper arrested his progress with both hands, and fixing his eyes on Fred's necktie, whispered,

"You don't think *I'm* to blame, do you?"

" Why—no—I don't see how, exactly," said Fred, endeavoring to escape.

" Fred," whispered the Squire, tightening his hold on the lapels of Fred's coat, " tell *him* so, won't you? I'll be your best friend forever if you will; it's dreadful to think of a man going up to God with such an idea on his mind, even if it *is* a mistake. Of course, when he gets there he'll find out he's wrong, *if* he is, as——"

Fred broke away from the storekeeper, and wedged himself between the doctor and pastor. Doughty withdrew his wrist from the doctor's fingers, extended a thin hand, and smiled.

" Fred," said he, " we used to be chums when we were boys. I never took an advantage of you, did I? "

" Never," said Fred ; " and we'll have lots of good times again, old fellow. I've just bought the best spring wagon in the State, and I'll drive you all over the country when you get well enough."

George's smile became slightly grim as he replied,

" I guess Barker's hearse is the only spring wagon I'll ever ride in again, my boy."

" Nonsense, George ! " exclaimed Fred heartily. " How many times have I seen you almost dead,

and then put yourself together again? Don't you
remember the time when you gave out in the mid-
dle of the river, and then picked yourself up, and
swam the rest of the way? Don't you remember
the time we got snowed in on Raccoon Mountain,
and we both gave up and got ready to die, and how
you not only came to, but dragged me home besides?
The idea of *you* ever dying! I wish you'd sent for
me when you first took the silly notion into your
head."

Doughty was silent for a moment; his eyes
brightened a little and a faint flush came to his
cheeks; he looked fondly at his wife, and then at
his children; he tried to raise himself in his bed;
but in a minute his smile departed, his pallor
returned, and he said, in the thinnest of voices,

" It's no use, Fred; in those days there was something in me to call upon at a pinch; now there
isn't a thing. I haven't any time to spare, Fred;
what I want to ask is, keep an eye on my boys, for
old acquaintance' sake. Their mother will be almost
everything to them, but she can't be expected to
know about their ways among men. I want somebody to care enough for them to see that they don't
make the mistakes I've made."

A sudden rustle and a heavy step was heard, and Squire Tomple approached the bedside, exclaiming,

" *I'll* do that! "

" Thank you, Squire," said George feebly ; " but you're not the right man to do it."

" George," said the Squire, raising his voice, and unconsciously raising his hand, " I'll give them the best business chances that can be had ; I can do it, for I'm the richest man in this town."

" You gave *me* the best chance in town, Squire, and this is what has come of it," said Doughty.

The Squire precipitately fell back and against his old place by the wall. Doughty continued,

" Fred, persuade them—tell them that I said so— that a business that makes them drink to keep up, isn't business at all—it's suicide. Tell them that their father, who was never drunk in his life, got whisky to help him use more of himself, until there wasn't anything left to use. Tell them that drinking for strength means discounting the future, and that discounting the future always means getting ready for bankruptcy."

" I'll do it, old fellow," said Fred, who had been growing very solemn of visage.

" They shan't ask you for any money, Fred,' explained Doughty, when the Squire's voice was again
heard saying,

" And they shan't refuse it from me."

" Thank you, Squire," said George. " I do think
you owe it to them, but I guess they've good enough
stuff in them to refuse it."

" George," said the Squire, again approaching
the bedside, " I'm going to continue your salary to
your wife until your boys grow big enough to help
her. You know I've got plenty of money—'twon't
hurt me; for God's sake make her promise to
take it."

" She won't need it," said Doughty. " My life's
insured."

" Then what *can* I do for her—for them—for
you?" asked the Squire. "George, you're holding
your—sickness—against me, and I want to make it
right. I can't say I believe I've done wrong by
you, but you think I have, and that's enough to
make me want to restore good feeling between us
before—in case anything should happen. Anything
that money *can* do, it *shall* do."

" Offer it to God Almighty, Squire, and buy my
life back again," said Doughty. "If you can't do

that, your money isn't good for anything in this house."

The doctor whispered to his patient that he must not exert himself so much; the Squire whispered to the doctor to know what else a man in his own position could do?

Fred Macdonald could think of no appropriate expression with which to break the silence that threatened. Suddenly Parson Wedgewell raised his head, and said,

" My dear young friend, this is a solemn moment. There are others who know and esteem you, beside those here present; have you no message to leave for them? Thousands of people rightly regard you as a young man of high character, and your influence for good may be powerful among them. I should esteem it an especial privilege to announce, in my official capacity, such testimony as you may be moved to make, and as your pastor, I feel like claiming this mournful pleasure as a right. What may I say ? "

" Say," replied the sick man, with an earnestness which was almost terrible in its intensity; " say that whisky was the best business friend I ever found, and that when it began to abuse me, no one thought

4*

enough of me to step in between us.   And tell them
that this story is as true as it is ugly."

As Doughty spoke, he had raised himself upon
one elbow ; as he uttered his last word, he dropped
upon his pillow, and passed into a land to which no
one but his wife manifested any willingness to follow him.

CHAPTER VIII.

AN ESTIMABLE ORGANIZATION CRITICISED.

THE funeral services of George Doughty were as largely attended as the great temperance meeting had been, and the attendants admitted—although the admission was not, logically, of particular force—that they received the worth of their money. The pall-bearers, twelve in number, were all young men who had been in the habit of drinking, but who had signed the pledge, some of them having appended signatures to special pledges privately prepared on the evening before the service. The funeral anthem was as doleful as the most sincere mourner could have wished, the music having been composed especially for the occasion by the chorister of Mr. Wedgewell's church. As for the sermon, it was universally voted the most powerful effort that Parson Wedgewell had ever made. Day and night had the good man striven with Doughty's parting injunction, determined to transmit the exact spirit of it, but horrified at its verbal

form. At last he honestly made George's own words
the basis of his whole sermon; his method being,
first, to show what would have been naturally the
last words of a young man of good birth and Christian breeding, and then presenting George's moral
legacy by way of contrast. To point the moral
without offending Squire Tomple's pride, and without inflicting useless pain upon the Squire's suffi-
ciently wounded heart, was no easy task; but the
parson was not lacking in tact and tenderness, so he
succeeded in making of his sermon an appeal so
powerful and all-applicable that none of the hearers found themselves at liberty to search out those
to whom the sermon might seem personally addressed.

Among the hearers was Mr. Crupp, and no one
seemed more deeply interested and affected. He
followed the funeral cortege to the cemetery; but,
arrived there, he halted at the gate, instead of following the example of the multitude by crowding
as closely as possible to the grave. The final services were no sooner concluded, however, than the
object of Mr. Crupp's unusual conduct became apparent to one person after another, the disclosure
being made to people in the order of their earthly

possessions. The parson was shocked at learning
that Mr. Crupp was importuning every man of
means to take stock in a woolen mill, to be established at Barton; but a whispered word or two from
Crupp caused the parson to abate his displeasure,
and finally to stand near Crupp's side and express
his own hearty approbation of the enterprise pro-
posed. Then Mr. Crupp whispered a few words
to Squire Tomple, and the Squire subscribed a
hundred shares at ten dollars each, information
of which act was disseminated among business
men and well-to-do farmers by Parson Wedgewell with an alacrity which, had modern business ideas prevailed at Barton, would have laid
the parson open to a suspicion of having accepted a few shares, to be paid for by his
own influence. Then Deacon Jones subscribed
twenty shares, and Judge Macdonald, Fred's father,
promised to take fifty; Crupp's name already stood
at the head of the list for a hundred. No stock-
company had ever been organized at Barton before,
and the citizens had always manifested a laudable
reluctance to allow other people to handle their
money; but this case seemed an exception to all
others; confidence in the enterprise was so power-

fully expressed, alike by the mercantile community,
the bar, the church, and the unregenerate (the last-
named class being represented by the ex-vender of
liquors), that people who had any money made
haste to participate in what seemed to them a race
for wealth with the odds in everybody's favor.
Crupp neglected no one; he scorned no subscription on account of its smallness; before he left the
cemetery gate nearly half the requisite capital had
been pledged, and before he slept that night he
found it necessary to accept rather more than the
twenty thousand dollars which, it had been decided
two days before, would be needed. Several days
later a board of directors was elected; two or three
of the directors informally offered the superintendency of the mill to Fred Macdonald, on condition
that he would pledge himself to abstain from the
use of intoxicating beverage while he held the
position, and then Fred was elected superintendent
in regular form and by unanimous vote of the board
of directors.

Great was the excitement in Barton and the
tributary country when it was announced that the
mill needed no more money, and that, consequently,
no more stock would be issued. In that myste-

rious way in which such things always happen, the secret escaped, and encountered every one, that his new position would prevent Fred Macdonald from drinking; non-stockholders had then the additional grievance that they had been deprived of taking any part in an enterprise for the good of a fellow-man, and all because the rich men of the village saw money in it. None of these injured ones dared to express their minds on this subject to Squire Tomple, to whom so many of them owed money, or to Judge Macdonald, who, in his family pride, would have laid himself liable to action by the grand jury, had any one suggested that his oldest son had ever been in any danger of becoming a drunkard. But to Mr. Crupp they did not hesitate to speak freely; Crupp owned no mortgages, no total abstainers owed him money; besides, he not only was not a .church member, but he had been in that most infernal of all callings, rum-selling. So it came to pass that when one day Crupp went into Deacon Jones's store for a dollar's worth of sugar, and was awaiting his turn among a large crowd of customers, Father Baguss constituted himself spokesman for the aggrieved faction, and said,

"It 'pears to me, Mr. Crupp, as if reformin' was a payin' business."

Crupp being human, was not saintly, so he flushed angrily, and replied,

"It *ought* to be, if the religion you re so fond of is worth a row of pins; but I don't know what you're driving at."

"Oh! of course you don't know," said Father Baguss; "but everybody else does. You don't expect to make any money out of that woolen mill, do you?"

"Yes I do, too," answered Crupp quickly. "I'll make every cent I can out of it."

"Just so," said Father Baguss, consoling himself with a bite of tobacco; "an' them that's borne the burden and heat of the day can plod along and not make a cent 'xcept by the hardest knocks. I've been one of the Sons of Temperance ever since I was converted, an' that's nigh onto forty year; I don't see why I don't get *my* sheer of the good things of this world."

"If you mean," said Crupp, with incomparable deliberation, "that my taking stock in the mill is a reward to me for dropping the liquor business, you're mightily mistaken. I'd have taken it all the same if anybody had put me up to it when I was in the liquor business."

"Yes," sighed Father Baguss, "like enough you would; as the Bible says, 'The children of this world are wiser in their generation than the children of light.' I can't help a-gettin' mad, though, to think it has to be so."

Two or three unsuccessful farmers lounging about the stove sighed sympathetically, but Crupp indulged in a sarcastic smile, and remarked,

"*I* always supposed it was because the children of light had got their treasure laid up in heaven, and were above such worldly notions."

The late sympathizers of Father Baguss saw the joke, and laughed with unkind energy, upon which the good old man straightened himself and exclaimed,

"The children of the kingdom have to earn their daily bread, I reckon; manna don't fall nowadays like it used to do for the chosen people."

"Exactly," said Crupp, "and them that ain't chosen people don't pick up their dinners without working for them either, without getting into jail for it. But, say! I didn't come in here to make fun of you, Father Baguss. If you want some of that mill stock so bad, I'll sell you some of mine—that is, if you'll go into temperance with all your might."

The old man seemed struck dumb for a moment but when he found his tongue, he made that useful member make up for lost time. " Go into temperance !" he shouted. " Did anybody ever hear the like of that ? I that's been a " Son " more'n half my life ; that's spent a hundred dollars—yes, more —in yearly dues ; that's been to every temperance meetin' that's ever been held in town, even when I've had rheumatiz so bad I could hardly crawl ; that kept the pledge even when I was out in the Black Hawk War, where the doctors themselves said that I *ort* to have drank ; that's plead with drinkers, and been scoffed an' reviled like my blessed Master for my pains ; that's voted for the Maine Liquor Law ; that's been dead agin lettin' Miles Dalling into the church because he brews beer for his own family drinkin', though he's a good enough man every other way, as fur as I can see ; I that went to see every member of our church, an' begged an' implored 'em not to sell our old meetin'-house to the feller that's since turned it into a groggery ; I to be told by a feller like you, that's got the guilt of uncounted drunkards on your soul——"

Crupp, with a very white face, advanced a step or two toward the old man; but the participator in the Black Hawk War was not to be frightened, especially when he was so excited as he was now; so he roared,

"Come on! come on! perhaps you want *my* blood on your soul, with all the others; but just let me tell you, it isn't easy to get!"

Crupp recovered himself and replied, "Father Baguss, all that you've done is very well in its way, but it wasn't going into temperance. You've been a first-rate talker, I know, but talk isn't cider. Why, there's been lots of men in my store after listenin' to one of your strong temperance speeches, and laughed about what they've heard. I've told them they ought to be ashamed of themselves—don't shake your head—I *have*, and all they'd say would be, 'Talk don't cost anything, Crupp.' But if you'd followed up your tongue with your brains, and most of all your pocket, not one of them chaps would have opened his head about you."

"Money!" exclaimed the old man; "didn't I tell you that division dues alone had cost me more'n a hundred dollars; not to speak of subscriptions to public meetin's?"

"And every cent that didn't go to pay 'division' expenses, that is—for keeping a lodge-room in shape for you to meet in, and such things—went to pay for more talk. Did you Sons of Temperance ever *buy* a man away from his whisky? It *might* have been done—done cheap too—in almost any week since I've been in Barton, by helping down-hearted men along. Did you ever do it yourself?"

Father Baguss was nonplused for a moment, noting which a bystander, also a Son of Temperance, came valiantly to the rescue of his order, by exclaiming,

"Tongues was made to use, and the better the cause, the more it needs to be talked about."

"There's no getting away from that," said Crupp. "Talk's all right in its place; but when anybody's sick in your family, you don't hire somebody to come in and talk him well, do you?"

The auxiliary replied by pressing perceptibly closer to the bale of blankets against which he had been leaning, and Crupp was enabled to concentrate his attention upon Father Baguss. But the old soldier had in his military days unconsciously acquired a tactical idea or two which were frequently applicable in real life. One of them was that of flanking, and he straightway attempted it by exclaiming,

"I'd use money quick enough on drunkards, if I saw anybody fit to use it on," said he; "it would do my old soul good to find a drinking man that I could be sure money would save. But they're a shiftless, worthless pack of shotes, all that I see of 'em. There *wuz* a young fellow—Lije Mason his name was—that I once thought seriously of doin' somethin' fur; but he went an' signed the pledge, an' got along all right by himself."

"But there's your own neighbors, old Tappelmine and his family—they all drink; what have you done for 'em?" asked Crupp.

"A lot of Kentucky poor white trash!" exclaimed Father Baguss. "What *could* anybody do for 'em? Besides, they do for 'emselves; they've stole hams out of my smoke-house more'n once, an' they know *I* know it, too."

"Poor white trash is sometimes converted in church, isn't it?" asked Mr. Crupp; "and what's to keep poor white trash from stopping drinking? what but a good, honest, religious, rum-hating neighbor that looks at 'em so savagely and lets 'em alone so hard that they'd take pains to get drunk, just to

worry him? I know how you feel toward them;
I *saw* it once: one Sunday I passed you on the road
just opposite their place; you was in your wagon
takin your folks to church, and I—well, I was out
trying to shoot a wild turkey, which I mightn't
have been on a Sunday. They were all laughin' and
cuttin' up in the house—it's seldom enough such
folks get anything to laugh about—and I could just
see you groan, and your face was as black as a thunder cloud, and as savage as an oak knot soaked in
vinegar. The old man came out just then for an
armful of wood, and nodded at you pleasant enough;
but that face of yours was too much for him, and
pretty soon he looked as if he'd have liked to throw
a chunk of wood at your head. I'd have *done* it, if
I'd been him. The old man was awfully drunk
when I came back that way, two or three hours
later. That was a pretty day's work for a Son of
Temperance, wasn't it—and Sunday, too?"

The casing to Father Baguss's conscience was not
as thick as that to his brain, and he was silent;
perhaps the prospect of getting some mill stock
aided the good work in his heart.

Crupp continued: "I'm a 'Son' myself, now, and
I know what a man agrees to when he joins a divi-

sion.   If you think you've lived up to it—you and
the other members of the Barton Division—I suppose you've a right to your opinion ; but if my ideas,
picked up on both sides of the fence, are worth anything to you, they amount to just this : the Sons
of Temperance in this town haven't done anything
but help each other not to get back into bad ways
again, and to give a welcomin' hand to anybody
that's strong enough in himself to come into the
division with you ; and that isn't the spirit of the
order."

Crupp got his sugar, and no one pressed him to
stay longer ; but, as he slowly departed, as became a
soldier who was not retreating but only changing
his base, Father Baguss followed him, touched his
sleeve as soon as he found himself outside the store
door, and said,

" Say, Crupp, I'll try to do something for Tappelmine, though I don't know yet what it'll be, an'
I don't care if you *do* let me have about five sheers
of that mill stock; I s'pose you won't want more
than you paid for it ? '

CHAPTER IX.

SOME VOLUNTEER SHEPHERDS.

THE mail-stage did not make its appearance at the usual hour on the day following Crupp's conversation with Father Baguss, and during a lull in the desultory conversation which prevailed among those who were waiting for the mail, the postmaster displayed at his window his large, round face, devoid of its habitual jolly smile, and remarked,

"Too bad about Wainright, isn't it?"

"What's that?" asked half a dozen at once.

The postmaster looked infinitely more important all in a second. It is but seldom in this world that a man can tell a bit of news to an assembled crowd; and in an inland town, before the day of the omnipresent telegraph pole, the chances were proportionately fewer than elsewhere. The postmaster had a generous heart, however, and at the risk of losing his importance he opened his treasure-house all at once:

"He's been pretty high on whiskey for two or

three days," said he, " and they say he's got snakes
in his boots now; anyhow, he's made a sudden
break for Louisville; he started on foot, an hour or
two ago, for Brown's Landing, seven miles below
here, to catch a down-river steamboat; he was clear-
headed enough to find out first that it wasn't likely
that the *Excellence*, that's about due, wouldn't
have any freight to stop for here. His wife's half
wild about it, but there's nothing the poor thing
can do."

" Poor, misguided man!" sighed Parson Wedgewell, who had arrived just in time to hear the story.
"The ways of Providence are undoubtedly wise,
but they are indeed mysterious. Judging according to our finite capacities, it would be natural to
suppose that capabilities so unusual as those of Mr.
Wainright would be divinely guided."

"I saw him coming down the walk," observed
Squire Tomple, "and I thought he looked rather
peculiar, so I just stepped across the street; I don't
like to get into a row with men in that fix."

" Of course getting into a row was the only thing
that could be done," said Crupp, who had apparently
been carefully reading a posted notice of a sheriff's
sale.

5

The Squire did not enjoy the tone in which Crupp's remark was delivered ; but before he could reason with the new reformer, the Reverend Timotheus Brown dashed into the fray in defense of a beloved idea, which the rival pastor had seemed covertly to assail.

" The reason such natures aren't divinely guided," said he, in a voice which suggested nutmeg-graters to the acute sensibilities of Parson Wedgewell, " is that they don't implicitly submit themselves to the Divine will."

" A man can do nothing unless the Spirit draw him," said Parson Wedgewell valiantly.

" That's rather hard on a fellow, though, isn't it ?'. soliloquized Fred Macdonald.

" Not a bit of it," spoke out Father Baguss, who had been scenting the battle from an inner room. " Bless the Lord ! the parables of the lost sheep that the shepherd left the rest of the flock to look for, and the lost coin that the woman hunted for, wasn't told for nothin'. The Lord knows how to 'tend to his own business."

" And nobody else can do a thing to help the Lord along, can he ? " said Crupp, passing his arm through the postmaster's window, and extracting

from his box a copy of the Louisville *Journal*
(then the only paper of prominence in a large sec-
tion of Western country) ; "all that men have to do
in such cases is just to talk."

Crupp departed, encountering on the way the
wide-open countenance of Tom Adams, who was
waiting for Deacon Jones's mail. The two pastors
preserved silence, that of Mr. Brown being extremely
dignified, with a visible trace of acerbity, while that
of Mr. Wedgewell was strongly suggestive of mental unquiet. The distribution of the small mail,
which had arrived soon after the conversation began,
gave everybody an excuse to depart—an excuse of
which most of them availed themselves at once,
Squire Tomple having first changed the direction
of the conversation by inquiring particularly of
Father Baguss as to the number and probable
weight of the porkers which the old man was fat-
tening for the winter market. The subject lasted
only until the two men reached the door, however,
and then each sympathized with the other over the
wounds received at the hands, or tongue, of the un-
sentimental and irreligious Crupp. Yet the more
they talked of Crupp, the less they seemed to realize
their pain.

4

Tom Adams went straight to his employer's store, and exclaimed, not in his usual ingenuous manner,

" Deacon, old Berry won't take that load of bricks unless he gets 'em right off; I guess I'll take 'em right out to him. It's a long trip, but there's three hours yet 'fore dark."

" Be sure you do, then, Thomas," said the deacon.

Tom was soon in his wagon, and going toward the brick-yard at a livelier rate than was consistent with the proper care of horses with a long, heavy pull before them. The bricks were loaded with apparent regard to count, but not in good order, and, as Tom followed the road to old Berry's, he soliloquized :

" I ort to be able to ketch him after I deliver the bricks, but what in thunder am I to say to him ? Like enough he'll knock me down if I don't look out. That's just the notion, I *de*-clare ! I can knock *him* down, and put him right in the wagon and bring him back; the joltin' would fetch him to and clear his head, like it's done mine often enough when I've been in his fix. But, hang it, what a ridick'lus goose-chase it does look like ! "

Meanwhile the Reverend Timotheus Brown had

limped down the main street, looking a little more
unapproachable than usual. As he reached the
edge of the town, however, where there began the
low plain which led to the river, he quickened his
pace somewhat, and he did not stop until he reached
the river. Upon a raft sat a man fishing, and near
by a canoe was tied; in this latter the preacher
seated himself, having first untied it.

"Hello, there! What are you a-doin' with my
dug-out?" shouted the fisherman.

"The Lord hath need of it!" roared the old
divine, picking up the paddle.

"Well, I'll be ——!" exclaimed the man; "if
that *ain't* the coolest! The Lord'll get a duckin',
I reckon, for that's the *wobbliest* canoe. I don't
know, though; the old fellow paddles as if he were
used to it."

Away down the river went the Reverend Timotheus; at the same time Fred Macdonald, on horseback, hailed the ferry-boat, crossed the river, and
galloped down the opposite bank, and Crupp, a
half an hour later, might have been seen lying on
his oars in a skiff in a shallow a mile above the
town, waiting to board the *Excellence*, as she came
down the stream.

"'Pears to me preachers are out for a walk to-day," said one old lady to another across a garden fence, in one edge of the town. "I saw Mr. Brown 'way down the street ever so far to-day, an' now here's Brother Wedgewell 'way out here. I thought like enough he was goin' to call, but he went straight along an' only bowed, awful solemn."

Parson Wedgewell certainly walked very fast, and the more ground he covered the more rapidly his feet moved, and not his feet only. In long stretches of road shut in by forest trees he found himself devoid of a single mental restraint, and he thought aloud as he walked.

"Rebuked by a sinner! O God! with my whole heart I have sought thee, and thou hast instead revealed thyself not only unto babes and sucklings, but unto one who is certainly not like unto one of these little ones. Teach me thy will, for verily in written books I fear I have found it not. What if the boat reaches the landing before I do, and this lost sheep escapes me? Father in Heaven, the shepherd is astray in his way, even as the sheep is; but O thou! who didst say that the race is not to the swift, nor the battle to the strong, make the feeble power of man to triumph over great engines

and the hurrying of mighty waters. Fulfill thy
promise, O God, for the sake of the soul thou hast
committed to my charge ! "

Then, like a man who believed in helping his own
prayers along, the parson snatched off his coat and
hat and increased his speed. He was far outside of
his own parish, for most of his congregation were
townsmen, and the old pastor knew no more of the
geography of the country about him than he did of
Chinese Tartary. He had taken what was known
as the " River Road," and thus far his course had
been plain ; now, however, he reached a place where
the road divided, and which branch to take he did
not know. Ordinary sense of locality would have
taught him in an instant, but the parson had no
such sense ; there was no house in sight at which he
could ask his way, and, to add to his anxiety, the
Excellence came down the river to his left and
rear, puffing and shrieking as if the making of
hideous noises was the principal qualification of a
river steamer. The old man fell upon his knees,
raised his face and hands toward heaven, and
exclaimed,

" The hosts of hell are pressing hard, O God !
Thou who didst guide thy chosen people with a pil-

lar of fire, show now to thy unworthy servant that thou art God!"

What the parson saw he never told, but he sprang to his feet and went down the left-hand road at a lively run, a moment after Tom Adams, half a mile in the rear, had shaded his eyes and exclaimed,

"Blamed if there isn't a feller a-prayin' right out in the road; if he wants anything *that* bad, I hope he'll get it.   Travel, Selim—*get* up, Bill!—let's see who he is."

CHAPTER X.

SPEAKING after the manner of the flesh, the Reverend Timotheus Brown had found only plain sailing on the river; spiritually, he had a very different experience. "As stubborn as a mule" was the most common of the current estimates of Pastor Brown's character; and if the conscientious old preacher had ever personally heard this opinion of himself, the verbal expression thereof would have given him but slight annoyance, compared with that which he experienced from his own inner man as he paddled down the stream. To forcibly resist something so satisfied the strongest demand of his nature that neither shortening breath nor blistering hands caused him to slacken the speed with which he forced his paddle against the water. But another contest was going on, and in this the consistent theologian was not so triumphant as he liked always to be. Harry Wainright was one of the ungodly; that he owned (and frequently occupied) a high-

priced pew in Mr. Brown's own church was only
another reason why the preacher should quote con-
cerning him, "He that being often reproved har-
deneth his neck ——"— what if the conclusion of
the same passage—"shall suddenly be destroyed,
and that without remedy," should apply? What
could prevent its doing so, if Wainright had fulfilled
the description in the first half? Had not the same
God inspired the whole passage? If so, what right
had any man, least of all a minister of the Gospel, to
try to set at naught the Divine will? Harry Wainright was, according to the decrees of an unchange-
able God, one of the lost—as much so as if he were
already in the bottomless pit. And still the old man's
paddle flew; once on the trip he had felt as if the
weakness of the arm of flesh would decide the case
for him, and in favor of the Word whose expounder
he was; he found himself wishing that it might, so
that he could feel that although God had overruled
him, he might have comfort in the assurance that
he had not proved indifferent to his sudden emotion
of yearning for his fellow man. But that mysterious
physical readjustment, known in animals as "second
breath," came to the rescue of his fainting frame,
and then it seemed as if no watery torrent could

prevail against the force of his arm. Oh! if he
might but talk to some one of the fathers of the
church; that he might be, even for ten minutes,
back in his own library! But no father of the
church resided along the Reverend Brown's nauti-
cal course, nor was there a theological library
nearer than his own, and there he was, actually bent
upon saving one whom the Eternal pronounced
lost! Lost? Hold! "For the Son of Man is
come into the world to save them that are lost." If
Christ had a right to save the lost, had not an ambassador of Christ the same privilege? was not an
ambassador one who stood in the place—who fulfilled the duties—of an absent king? "Glory be to
God on high!" shouted the Reverend Timotheus,
and the dense woods echoed back "God on high!"
as the old man, forty years a conscientious pastor,
but only that instant converted to Christianity,
drove his paddle into the water with a force that
nearly threw the canoe into the air.

As for Parson Wedgewell, whom we left arising
from his knees after asking information from his
Divine guide, he found himself upon the right road.
The river was nearer than he had dared to hope; a run
of half a mile brought him into a clearing, in which

stood Brown's warehouse, near the river. The *Excellence* had just put her nose against the bank, and
the clerk at the warehouse was tired of wondering
why Fred Macdonald, on the opposite bank, was
shouting so impatiently to the ferryman, and why
an old man in a canoe should be coming down the
river at the rate of fifty-paddle strokes per minute,
when he saw Parson Wedgewell, coatless, hatless,
with open shirt, disordered hair, and face covered
with dirt deposited just after an unlucky stumble,
come flying along the road, closely followed by Tom
Adams, who was lashing his horses furiously. A
happy inspiration struck the clerk; he shouted
" Horse thief! " and seized the parson, and instantly
received a blow under the chin which rendered him
inactive and despondent for the space of half an
hour. The parson saw the gang-plank shoved out ;
he saw Harry Wainright step aboard ; he saw the
Rev. Timotheus jump from his canoe into water
knee deep, dash up the plank, and throw his arm
over Harry Wainright's shoulder ; but only a second
or two elapsed before Parson Wedgewell monopo-
lized the runaway's other side, and then, as the
three men stared at each other, neither one speaking a word, and the two pastors bursting into

tears, Tom Adams hurried aboard, and exclaimed,

"Mr. Wainright, Mrs. Wainright is particular
anxious to see you this evenin', for somethin', I
don't know what, an' I hadn't time to get any sort
of a carriage for fear I'd lose the boat; but there's
good springs to the seat of the brick-yard wagon, an'
a new sheep-skin besides." No other words coming
to Tom's mind, he abruptly walked forward muttering, "That's the cock-an'-bullest yarn I ever *did*
tell; I *knew* I wouldn't know what to say." As Tom
meditated, he heard one "roustabout" say to another,

"I say, Bill, you know that feller that used to sell
such bully whiskey in Barton? Well, he's around
there on the guards, dancin' like a lunatic. I
shouldn't wonder if that's what come of swearin' off
drinkin'."

"Mighty unsafe perceedin'," replied Bill, eyeing
Crupp suspiciously.

Harry Wainright made not the slightest objection
to going back home, and he acted very much like a
man who was glad of the company in which he
found himself. The divine of the canoe looked at
his blistered hands, and paid the resuscitated clerk

3*

to send the boat back by the first steamer. While Fred Macdonald was crossing the river, Tom Adams kindly drove back the road and recovered Parson Wedgewell's coat and hat, and the parson accepted the hospitalities of the boat to the extent of water, soap, and towel. He attempted to make his peace with the injured clerk; but that functionary, having already interviewed Tom Adams, insisted that no apology was necessary, and asked the old gentleman in what church he preached.

As the party started back, they saw, coming through a cross-road, a buggy violently driven, and containing two men—who proved to be Squire Tomple and Father Baguss—in a vehicle belonging to the latter; their air of having merely happened there deceived no one, least of all Harry Wainright himself. Father Baguss did not live in town, nor within four miles of it; but when Squire Tomple suggested that he would beg a ride back in Tom Adams's wagon, Father Baguss objected, and remarked that he guessed he had business in town himself; so the Squire retained his seat, and Father Baguss fell in behind the wagon as decorously as if he was taking part in a funeral procession. Behind them came Fred Macdonald, who had good excuse

to gallop back to the peculiar attraction that
awaited him in Barton, but preferred to remain in
his present company. As the party approached the
town, Tom Adams considerately drove through the
darkest and most unfrequented streets, and stopped
as near as possible to Wainright's house. Wainright,
politely declining any escort, walked quietly home.
Father Baguss stood up in his buggy, with his hand
to his ear, in the original position of attention :
suddenly he exclaimed,

"There! I heard his door shut: *now*, brethren." And Father Baguss started the doxology.
"Praise God from whom all blessings flow," and
the glorious harmonies of the old choral were
proof even against the tremendous but discordant
notes which Tom Adams, with the most honorable
intentions, interjected in rapid succession. Then
the party broke up. The two pastors escorted each
other home alternately and several times in succession, during which apparently meaningless pro-
ceeding they learned, each from the other, how
much of good intent had been stifled in both of
them for lack of prompt application. Crupp and
Tomple talked but little, and no "Imaginary Conversation" would be at all likely to reproduce what

they said.   Father Baguss made the whole air
between Barton and his own farm redolent of camp-
meeting airs, and Fred Macdonald heard in Parson
Wedgewell's parlor something sweeter than all the
music ever written.   As for Tom Adams, he jogged
slowly toward his employer's stables, repeating to
himself,

"The bulliest spree I ever went on—the *very*
bulliest!"

CHAPTER XI.

DOCTORS AND BOYS.

THERE were two elements of Barton society with which Mr. Crupp had not been so successful as he had hoped ; these were the doctors, and that elastic body known as " the boys." Individually, the physicians had promised well at first; all of them but one were members of the Barton Division of the Sons of Temperance, and the Division rooms afforded the only floor upon which Dr. White, the allopathist, Dr. Perry, the homœopathist, and Dr. Pykem, the water-cure physician, ever could meet amicably, for they belonged to separate churches. Old Dr. Matthews, who had retired from practice, was not a " Son," only because he was a conscientious opponent of secret societies ; but he had signed every public pledge ever circulated in Barton, and he had never drunk a drop of liquor in his life. All the physicians freely admitted to Mr. Crupp that alcohol was a never-failing cause of disease, or

at least of physical deterioration ; all declared that
no class of maladies were so incurable, and so depressing to the spirits of the medical practitioner,
as those to which habitual drinkers, even those who
were never drunk, were subject; but—they really did
not see what more they, the physicians of Barton,
could do than they were already doing. Crupp discussed the matter with Parson Wedgewell, and the
parson volunteered to preach a sermon to physicians
from the text, " Give wine unto those that be of
heavy hearts," a text which had suggested itself to
him, or, rather, had been providentially suggested to
him on the occasion of his very first interview with
Crupp, and which was outlined in his mind in a manner suggestive of delightful subtleties and a startling
application. But when Crupp sounded the doctors as
to whether such a discourse would be agreeable, Dr.
White said he would be glad to listen to the eloquent divine ; but he was conscientiously opposed to
appearing, even by the faintest implication, to admit that the homeopathist was a physician at all.
Dr. Perry felt his need, as a partaker in the fall of
Adam, to being preached to from any portion of
the inspired Word ; but he could not sit in an audience to which such a humbug as Pykem could be

admitted in an official capacity; while Dr. Pykem
said that he would rejoice to encourage the preacher
by his presence, if he thought any amount of preaching would do any good to a remorseless slaughterer
like White, or an idiotic old potterer like Perry.
Then Mr. Crupp tried another plan: he himself organized a meeting in which the exercises were to
consist of short addresses upon the physical bearing
of intemperance, the addresses to be made by " certain of our fellow-citizens who have had many op-
portunities for special observation in this direction."
Even then Drs. White and Perry objected to sitting
on the same platform with Dr. Pykem, who had
never attended any medical school of any sort, and
who would probably say something utterly ridicu-
lous in support of his own senseless theories, and
thus spoil the effect of the physiological facts and
deductions which Drs. Perry and White each admitted that the other might be intellectually capable
of advancing. Crupp arranged the matter amicably,
however, by having Pykem make the first address,
during which the other two physicians were to
occupy back seats, where they might, while unob-
served, take notes of such of Pykem's heresies as
they might deem it necessary to combat : he further

arranged that, immediately after Pykem had concluded, he was to be called away to a patient, provided
for the occasion. Still more—and great would have
been the disgust of White and Perry had they known
of it—Crupp laid so plainly before Pykem the necessities of the community, and the duty, not only
Christian, but of the simplest manliness, also, that
men of any intelligence owed to their fellow-men,
that Pykem, who with all his hobbies was a man of
Christian belief and humane heart, confined himself
solely to the preventive efficacy of external appli-
cations of water, not unmixed with soap, in the case
of persons who felt toward alcohol a craving which
they could not logically explain ; he thus delivered
an address which might, with cause, be repeated in
every community in the United States. Then Dr.
Perry, whose forte was experimental physiology, read
whole tables of statistics based upon systematic ob-
servations ; and Dr. White unrolled and explained
some charts and plates of various internal organs,
naturally unhandsome in themselves, which had
been injured by alcohol. It was declared by close
observers that for a few days after this meeting the
demand for sponges and toilet soap exceeded the experience of the old and single apothecary of the

village, and that liquor-sellers looked either sober or savage, according to their respective natures.

But the boys! Crupp found himself in time really disposed to ask Pastors Wedgewell and Brown whether there wasn't Scriptural warrant for the supposition that Job obtained his sons by marrying a widow with a grown-up family. "The boys" numbered about a hundred specimens, ranging in age from fourteen years to forty; no two were alike in disposition, as Crupp had long known; they came from all sorts of peculiar social conditions that warred against their physical and moral well-being; some of them seemed wholly corrupt, and bent upon corrupting others; many more exhibited a faculty for promising which could be matched in magnitude only by their infirmity of performance. By a vigorous course of individual exhortation, the burden of which was that everybody knew they drank because they were too cowardly to refuse, and that nobody despised them so heartily as the very men who sold them the rum, Crupp lessened the number of drinking boys by about one-fourth, thus rescuing those who were easiest to save and most worth saving, but the remainder made as much trouble as the collective body had done. Crupp

scolded, pleaded, and argued; he hired some boys
to drop liquor for at least a stated time; he impor-
tuned some of the more refined citizens to interest
themselves socially in certain boys; he lent some
of these boys money with which to buy clothing
which would bring their personal appearance up
to the Barton standard of respectability, and he
covertly excited some of the merchants up to a
genuine interest in certain boys, by persuading them
to sell to said boys coats, boots, and hats on credits
nominally short.

He enjoyed the hearty co-operation of the village
pastors, all of whom preached sermons to young
men and to parents; but his principal practical
assistance came, quite unexpectedly, from old Bunley. Bunley had not yet succeeded in finding anything to do, and, as he had on his hands all of his
time which was not needed at the family woodpile,
he went around talking to the boys. Bunley had
been, according to the Barton classification, a " boy "
himself; he had drunk in a not remote day with
any boy who invited him; he knew more jolly songs
than any other half dozen inebriates in the village,
and was simply oppressed with the load of good
(bad) stories which he never tired of telling; he had

been always ready to play cards with any boy, and
had come to be regarded, among the youngsters, as
" the best fellow in the village."   Now that he had
reformed, his success in reforming boys was simply
remarkable—so much so that Parson Wedgewell
began to tremble over the thought that Bunley, by
the present results of the experience of his sinful
days, might demonstrate, beyond the hope of refuta-
tion, the dreadful proposition that it was better that
a man should be a sinner in his youth, so as to know
how to be a saint when he became old.   This idea
Parson Wedgewell laid, with much trepidation,
before the Reverend Timotheus Brown, and the two
old saints and new friends had a delightfully doleful time on their knees over it, until there occurred
to the Reverend Timotheus Brown a principle which
he proceeded to formulate as follows :   The greater
the capacity of a misguided faculty for evil, the
greater the good the same faculty may accomplish
when in its normal condition.   To be sure, the dis-
covery was not original with him ; the same state-
ment had been made by peripatetic phrenologists at
Barton ; indeed, it was visible, to one who could
read rather than merely repeat words, in every chapter of the Bible so dear to this good old man ; but

the illusion under which Parson Brown was allowed
to labor worked powerfully for his own good and for
that of the community, for from that time forth
both he and Parson Wedgewell displayed their
greatest earnestness in work with cases apparently
the most hopeless. These they found among " the
boys," and harder work no reformer ever laid
out for himself. The ingenuity, the persistence, the
determined brutality of some of the boys, the logi-
cal acuteness displayed in varied fits of deception,
only stimulated the old man to greater industry,
and slowly, after hard work, often after work that
seemed more like hard fighting, but yet surely,
Parson Brown reformed one after another of several
hard cases. The villagers, most of whom considered
that their whole duty consisted in critical observation, applauded handsomely, and Bunley was astonished, and felt considerably mortified at the marked
success of his new rival, while Parson Wedgewell
found it necessary to pray earnestly that unchristian
jealousy might be banished from his own mind.
But to Parson Brown the greatest triumph occurred
when Crupp—Crupp, the literalist, the hard-headed,
the man who trusted in the arm of flesh, the man
of action, he who slightingly received any sugges-

tions of special thank-offerings of prayer for special services received—Crupp came to him by night—it reminded Parson Brown of Nicodemus—and exclaimed, " It's no use, Parson ; I've done my best on Frank Pughger, but he's a goner if God don't put in a special hand.   I'll turn him over to you, I guess."

CHAPTER XII.

TWO SIDES OF A CLOUD.

THE holy hilarity which Father Baguss enjoyed on his way home, after having assisted in bringing Harry Wainright back, did not depart with the shades of night. The old man was out of bed at his usual hour, and he took his spiritual songs to the barn with him, to the astonishment of his mild-eyed cows and quick-eared horses; and when his drove of porkers demanded their morning meal with the vocal power peculiar to a chorus of swine, the old man defiantly jumped an occasional octave, and made the spiritual songs dominate over the physical. He seemed *so* happy that his single hired man could not resist the temptation of asking for an increase of pay; but the sobriety to which this interruption and its consequent refusal reduced Father Baguss was of only temporary duration, and the broken strain was resumed with renewed energy. The ecstasy lasted into and through the old man's matutinal repast, and manifested itself by

an occasional hum through the good man's nose,
which did the duty ordinarily performed by a
mouth which was now busied about other things;
it caused Father Baguss to read a glorious psalm
as he officiated at the family altar after breakfast;
it made itself felt half way through the set prayer
which the old farmer had delivered every morning
for forty years; but it seemed suddenly to depart as
its whilom possessor uttered the petition, "May
we impart to others of the grace with which thou
hast visited us so abundantly." For the Tappelmines had come suddenly into Father Baguss's
mind, and as that receptacle was never particularly
crowded, the Tappelmines made themselves very
much at home there. The prayer having ended,
the old man loitered about the house instead of
going directly to the "clearing," in which he had
been getting out some oak fence-rails; he stared
out of the window, walked up and down the kitchen
with his hands in his pockets, lit a pipe, relit it half
a dozen times at two minute intervals, sighed,
groaned, and at length strode across the room like
a bandit coming upon the boards of a theater,
seized his hat, and started for the Tappelmine domi-
cile.

4*

As he plodded along over the rough road, he had two very distinct ideas in his mind: one was, that he hadn't the slightest notion of what to say to Tappelmine; the other, and stronger, was, that it would be a relief to him to discover that Tappelmine was away from home, or even sick in bed—yes, or even drunk. But this hope was of very short duration, for soon the old man heard the Tappelmine axe, and, as he rounded the corner of the miserable house, he saw Tappelmine himself—a tall, gaunt figure in faded homespun, torn straw hat, and a tangled thicket of muddy-gray hair. The face which Tappelmine turned, as he heard the approaching footsteps, was not one to warm the heart of a man inspired only by an unwelcome sense of duty; it was thin, full of vagrant wrinkles; the nose had apparently started in different directions, and each time failed to return to its original line; the eyes were watery and colorless, and the lips were thin and drawn into the form of a jagged volcano crater.

"The idee of doin' anything for such!" exclaimed Father Baguss under his breath. "O Lord! *you* put me up to this here job—unless it was all Crupp's work; now see me through!" Then he said,

" How are you, neighbor ? "

" Oh ! off an' on, 'bout as usual," said Tappelmine, with a look which seemed to indicate that his
usual condition was not one upon which he was
particularly to be felicitated.

" How'd your crop turn out? " asked Father
Baguss, well knowing that " crop " was a terribly
sarcastic word to apply to the acre or two of badly
cultivated corn which Tappelmine had planted,
but yet feeling a frantic need of talking against
time.

" Well, not over'n above good," said Tappelmine,
as impervious to the innocent sarcasm as he would
have been to anything but a bullet or a glass of
whiskey. " I dunno what would have 'come of us
ef I hadn't knocked over a couple of deer last week."

" You might have given a hint to your neighbors,
if worst had come to worst," suggested Father
Baguss, perceiving a gleam of light, but not so
delighted over it as a moment or two before he had
expected to be. " Nobody'd have stood by an'
seen you starve."

" Glad you told me," said Tappelmine, abruptly
raising his axe, and starting two or three large
chips in quick succession.

The light seemed suddenly to be departing, and Father Baguss made a frantic clutch at it.

"You needn't have waited to be told," said he. "You know well enough we're all human bein's about here."

"Well," said Tappelmine, leaning on his axe, and taking particular care not to look into his neighbor's eye, "I used to borry a little somethin'—corn, mebbe, or a piece of meat once in a while; but folks didn't seem over an' above glad to lend 'em, an' I'm one of the kind of fellows that can take a hint, I am."

"That was 'cause you never said a word 'bout payin' back—leastways, you didn't at *our* house."

Tappelmine did not reply, except by looking sullen, and Father Baguss continued:

"Besides, it's kinder discouragin' to lend to a feller that gets tight a good deal—gets tight sometimes, anyhow; it's hard enough to get paid by folks that always keep straight."

As Tappelmine could say nothing to controvert this proposition, he continued to look sullen, and Father Baguss, finding the silence insupportably annoying, said rather more than he had intended to say. There are natures which, while containing

noble qualities, are most awkward expositors of
themselves, and that of Baguss was one of this
sort. Such people are given to action which is
open to criticism on every side; yet, in spite of
their awkwardnesses, they find in their weakness the source of whatever strength they discover
themselves to be possessed of. Father Baguss was
one of this special division of humanity; but—
perhaps for his own good—he was unconscious
of his strength and painfully observant of his weakness. Yet he continued as follows:

"Look here, Tappelmine, I came over here on
purpose to find out if I could do anything to help
you get into better habits. You don't amount to a
row of pins as things are now, and I don't like it ;
it's throwed up to me, because I'm your neighbor,
and there's folks that stick to it that *I'm* to blame.
I don't see how ; but if there's any cross layin'
around that fits my shoulders, I s'pose I ought to
pick it up an' pack it along. Now, why in creation
don't you give up drinkin,' an' go to church, an'
make a crop, an' do other things like decent folks
do? You're bigger'n I am, an' stouter, an' your
farm's as good as mine if you'd only work it. Now
why you don't do it, I don't see."

" Don't, eh?" snarled Tappelmine, dropping his axe, and leaning against the house with folded hands. "Well, 'cause I hain't got any plow, nor any harrow, nor but one hoss, nor rails enough to keep out cattle, nor seed-corn or wheat, nor money to buy it with, nor anything to live on until the crop's made, nor anything to prevent the crop when it's made from being grabbed by whoever I owe money to; *that's* why I don't make a crop. An' I don't go to church, 'cause I hain't got any clothes excep' these 'uns that I've got on, an' my wife's as bad off as *I* be. An' I don't give up drinkin', 'cause drinkin' makes me feel good, an' the only folks I know that care anything for me drink too. You fellers that only drink on the sly ——"

"I never touched a drop in all my life!" roared Father Baguss.

" That's right," said Tappelmine; "stick to it; there's some that'll believe that yarn. But what I was goin' to say was, folks that drink on the sly know it's comfortin', an' I don't see what they go a-pokin' up fellers that does it fair an' square for."

Father Baguss groaned, and some influence— the old man in later days laid it upon the arch-enemy of souls—suggested to him the foolishness of naving gone into so great an operation without first counting the cost ; hadn't the great Founder of the old man's religious faith enjoined a counting of the cost of any enterprise before entering upon it ? Father Baguss wished *that* chapter of Holy Writ might have met his eye that morning at the family altar ; but it had not, and, worse yet, Tappelmine was becoming wide awake and excited. It was not what the drunkard had said about drinking or church-going that troubled this would-be reformer ; Tappelmine's outline of his material condition was what annoyed Father Baguss; for, in spite of an occasional attempt to mentally allay his fears by falling back upon prayer, the incentive with which he had called upon Tappelmine had taken strong hold of his conscience, and persisted in making its influence felt. Plows and prayers, harrows and hopes, seed-corn and the seed sown by the wayside mixed themselves inextricably in his mind, as parallels often do when men dream, or when they are confronted by an emergency beyond the control of their own intellects. The old man prayed silently and earnestly for relief, and his prayer was answered in a manner not entirely according to his liking, for he felt moved to say,

"*I'll* lend you seed, if you'll go to work an' put it right in, an' I'll lend you a plow and a team to break up the ground with—I mean, I'll hire 'em to you, an' agree to buy your crop at rulin' price, an' pay you the difference in cash."

"That sounds somethin' like," remarked Tappelmine, thrusting his hands into his trowsers' pockets, and making other preparations for a business talk; "but," he continued, "what am I to live on along till harvest? 'Tain't even winter yet." ⌐

Father Baguss groaned, and asked, "What was you a-goin' to live on if I hadn't offered seed and tools, Tappelmine?"

"The Lord knows," answered the never-do-well, with unimpeachable veracity.

"Then," said the old farmer, "I guess he knows what you'll do in t'other case. You can work, I reckon. *I* hain't got much to do, but you can do it, at whatever prices is goin,' an' that'll help you get work of other folks; nobody can say I get stuck on the men I hire. So they're generally glad enough to hire 'em themselves."

Tappelmine did not seem overjoyed at his prospects, but he had the grace to say that they were better than he had expected. Father Baguss went home, feeling but little more comfortable than when he had started on his well-intended mission. Tappelmine sauntered into his own cabin, wondering how much of the promised seed-corn and wheat he could smuggle into town and trade for whiskey; but he was rather surprised to have his wife, a short, thin, sallow, uninteresting-looking woman, who had been listening at the broken window, approach him, throw her arms about his neck, and exclaim,

" Now, old man, we can be respectable, can't we? The chance has been a long time a-comin', but we've got it now."

The surprise was too great for Tappelmine, and he spent the remainder of the day in nursing his knee on the single hearthstone of his mansion. He was not undisturbed, however, and as men of his mental caliber hate persistent reason even worse than they do work, Mrs. Tappelmine not only coaxed her lord into resolving to be respectable, but allowed that gentleman to persuade himself that he had formed the resolution of his own accord.

CHAPTER XIII.

A PHENOMENON IN EMBRYO.

THE superintendency of the Mississippi Valley Woolen Mills was a position which exactly suited Fred Macdonald, and it gave him occasion for the expenditure of whatever superfluous energy he found himself possessed of, yet it did not engross his entire attention. The faculty which the busiest of young men have for finding time in which to present themselves, well clothed and unbusiness-like, to at least one young woman, is as remarkable and admirable as it is inexplicable. The evenings which did not find Fred in Parson Wedgewell's parlor were few indeed, and if, when he was with Esther, he did not talk quite as sentimentally as he had done in the earlier days of his engagement, and if he talked business very frequently, the change did not seem distasteful to the lady herself. For the business of which he talked was, in the main, of a sort which loving women have for ages recognized as the inevitable, and to which they have subjected them-

selves with a unanimity which deserves the grati-
tude of all humanity. Fred talked of a cottage
which he might enter without first knocking at the
door, and of a partnership which should be un-
limited; if he learned, in the course of successive
conversations, that even in partnerships of the most
extreme order many compromises are absolutely
necessary, the lesson was one which improved his
character in the ratio in which it abased his pride.
The cottage grew as rapidly as the mill, and on his
returns from various trips for machinery there came
with Fred's freight certain packages which prevented
their owner from appearing so completely the ab-
sorbed business man which he flattered himself that
he seemed.   Then the partnership was formed one
evening in Parson Wedgewell's own church, in the
presence of a host of witnesses, Fred appearing as
self-satisfied and radiant as the gainer in such trans-
actions always does, while Esther's noble face and
drooping eyes showed beyond doubt who it was
that was the giver.

As the weeks succeeded each other after the
wedding, however, no acquaintance of the couple
could wonder whether the gainer or the giver was
the happier. Fred improved rapidly, as the school-

boy improves ; but Esther's graces were already of mature growth, and rejoiced in their opportunity for development. Though she could not have explained how it happened, she could not but notice that maidens regarded her wonderingly, wives contemplated her wistfully, frowns departed and smiles appeared when she approached people who were usually considered prosaic. Yet shadows sometimes stole over her face, when she looked at certain of her old acquaintances, and the cause thereof soon took a development which was anything but pleasing to her husband.

"Fred," said Esther one evening, " it makes me real unhappy sometimes to think of the good wives there are who are not as happy as I am. I think of Mrs. Moshier and Mrs. Crayme, and the only reason that I can see is, their husbands drink."

"I guess you're right, Ettie," said Fred. "They didn't begin their domestic tyranny in advance, as *you* did—bless you for it."

"But why *don't* their husbands stop?" asked Esther, too deeply interested in her subject to notice her husband's compliment. "They must see what they're doing, and how cruel it all is."

"They're too far gone to stop ; I suppose that's

the reason," said Fred. " It hasn't been easy work for *me* to keep my promise, Ettie, and I'm a young man ; Moshier and Crayme are middle-aged men, and liquor is simply necessary to them."

" That dreadful old Bunley wasn't too old to reform, it seems," said Esther. " Fred, I believe one reason is that no one has asked them to stop. See how good Harry Wainright has been since he found that so many people were interested in him that day ! "

" Ye——es," drawled Fred, evidently with a suspicion of what was coming, and trying to change the subject by suddenly burying himself in his memorandum book. But this ruse did not succeed, for Esther crossed the room to where Fred sat, placed her hands on his shoulders, and a kiss on his forehead, and exclaimed,

" Fred, *you're* the proper person to reform those two men ! "

" Oh, Ettie," groaned Fred, " you're entirely mistaken. Why, they'd laugh right in my face, if they didn't get angry and knock me down. Reformers want to be older men, better men, men like your father, for instance, if people are to listen to them."

" Father says they need to be men who understand

the nature of those they are talking to," replied
Esther; "and you once told me that you understood Moshier and Crayme perfectly."

" But just think of what they are, Ettie," pleaded
Fred. " Moshier is a contractor, and Crayme's a
steamboat captain; *such* men never reform, though
they always are good fellows. Why, if I were to
speak to either of them on the subject, they'd laugh
in my face, or curse me. The only way I was able
to make peace with them for stopping drinking myself was to say that I did it to please my wife."

" Did they accept that as sufficient excuse? "
asked Esther.

" Yes," said Fred reluctantly, and biting his lips
over this slip of his tongue.

" Then you've set them a good example, and I
can't believe its effect will be lost," said Esther.

"I sincerely hope it won't," said Fred, very willing to seem a reformer at heart ; " nobody would be
gladder than I to see those fellows with wives as
happy as mine seems to be."

" Then why don't you follow it up, Fred, dear,
and make sure of your hopes being realized? You
can't imagine how much happier *I* would be if I
could meet those dear women without feeling that I

had to hide the joy that's so hard to keep to myself."

The conversation continued with considerable strain to Fred's amiability; but his sophistry was no match for his wife's earnestness, and he was finally compelled to promise that he would make an appeal to Crayme, with whom he had a business engagement, on the arrival of Crayme's boat, the *Excellence*.

Before the whistles of the steamer were next heard, however, Esther learned something of the sufferings of would-be reformers, and found cause to wonder who was to endure most that Mrs. Crayme should have a sober husband, for Fred was alternately cross, moody, abstracted, and inattentive, and even sullenly remarked at his breakfast-table one morning that he shouldn't be sorry if the *Excellence* were to blow up, and leave Mrs. Crayme to find her happiness in widowhood. But no such luck befell the lady: the whistle-signals of the *Excellence* were again heard in the river, and the nature of Fred's business with the captain made it unadvisable for Fred to make an excuse for leaving the boat unvisited.

It *did* seem to Fred Macdonald as if everything

conspired to make his task as hard as it could possibly be. Crayme was already under the influence of more liquor than was necessary to his well-being, and the boat carried as passengers a couple of men, who, though professional gamblers, Crayme found very jolly company when they were not engaged in their business calling. Besides, Captain Crayme was running against time with an opposition boat which had just been put upon the river, and he appreciated the necessity of having the boat's bar well stocked and freely opened to whoever along the river was influential in making or marring the reputation of steamboats. Fred finally got the captain into his own room, however, and made a freight contract so absent-mindedly that the sagacious captain gained an immense advantage over him ; then he acted so awkwardly, and looked so pale, that the captain suggested chills, and prescribed brandy. Fred smiled feebly, and replied,

" No, thank you, Sam ; brandy's at the bottom of the trouble. I "—here Fred made a tremendous attempt to rally himself—" I want *you* to swear off, Sam."

The astonishment of Captain Crayme was marked enough to be alarming at first ; then the ludicrous feature of Fred's request struck him so forcibly that he burst into a laugh before whose greatness Fred trembled and shrank.

"Well, by thunder!" exclaimed the captain, when he recovered his breath; "if that isn't the best thing I ever heard yet! The idea of a steamboat captain swearing off his whiskey! Say, Fred, don't you want me to join the church? I forgot that you'd married a preacher's daughter, or I wouldn't have been so puzzled over your white face to-day. Sam Crayme brought down to cold water! Wouldn't the boys along the river get up a sweet lot of names for me—the 'Cold-water Captain,' 'Psalm-singing Sammy'! and then, when an editor or any other visitor came aboard, *wouldn't* I look the thing, hauling out glasses and a pitcher of water! Say, Fred, does your wife let you drink tea and coffee?"

"Sam!" exclaimed Fred, springing to his feet, "if you don't stop slanting at my wife, I'll knock you down."

"Good!" said the captain, without exhibiting any signs of trepidation. "*Now* you talk like yourself again. I beg your pardon, old fellow; you know I was only joking, but it *is* too funny. You'll have to take a trip or two with me again, though, and be reformed."

" Not any," said Fred, resuming his chair; "take your wife along, and reform yourself."

" Look here, now, young man," said the captain, "*you're* cracking on too much steam.   Honestly, Fred, I've kept a sharp eye on you for two or three months, and I am right glad you can let whiskey alone.   I've seen times when I wished I were in your boots; but steamboats can't be run without liquor, however it may be with woolen mills."

" That's all nonsense," said Fred.   " You get trade because you run your boat on time, charge fair prices, and deliver your freight in good order. Who gives you business because you drink and treat ? "

The captain, being unable to recall any shipper of the class alluded to by Fred, changed his course.

" 'Tisn't so much that," said he ; " it's a question of reputation.   How would I feel to go ashore at Pittsburg or Louisville or Cincinnati, and refuse to drink with anybody ?   Why, 'twould ruin me. It's different with you who don't have to meet anybody but religious old farmers.   Besides, you've just been married."

"And you've been married for five years," said Fred, with a sudden sense of help at hand. " How do you suppose *your* wife feels?"

Captain Crayme's jollity subsided a little, but with only a little hesitation he replied,

" Oh ! she's used to it ; she doesn't mind it."

' You're the only person in town that thinks so, Sam," said Fred.

Captain Crayme got up and paced his little stateroom two or three times, with a face full of uncertainty. At last he replied,

" Well, between old friends, Fred, I don't think so very strongly myself. Hang it ! I wish I'd been brought up a preacher, or something of the kind, so I wouldn't have had business ruining my chances of being the right sort of a family man. Emily *don't* like my drinking, and I've promised to look up some other business ; but 'tisn't easy to get out of steamboating when you've got a good boat and a first-rate trade. Once she felt so awfully about it that I *did* swear off—don't tell anybody, for God's sake ! but I did. I had to look out for my character along the river, though ; so I swore off on the sly, and played sick. I'd give my orders to the mates and clerks from my bed in here, and then I'd

lock myself in, and read novels and the Bible to
keep from thinking. 'Twas awful dry work all
around ; but 'whole hog or none' is *my* style, you
know. There was fun in it, though, to think of
doing something that no other captain on the river
ever did. But, thunder ! by the time night came, I
was so tired of loafing that I wrapped a blanket
around my head and shoulders, like a Hoosier,
sneaked out the outer door here, and walked the
guards, between towns ; but I was so frightened for
fear some one would know me that the walk did me
more harm than good. And blue ! why a whole
cargo of indigo would have looked like a snow-storm
alongside of my feelings the second day ; 'pon my
word, Fred, I caught myself crying in the afternoon,
just before dark, and I couldn't find out what for
either. I tell *you*, I was scared, and things got
worse as time spun along ; the dreams I had that
night made me howl, and I felt worse yet when
daylight came along again. Toward the next night
I was just afraid to go to sleep ; so I made up my
mind to get well, go on duty, and dodge everybody
that it seemed I ought to drink with. Why, the
Lord bless your soul ! the first time we shoved off
from a town, I walked up to the bar, just as I always

did after leaving towns; the barkeeper set out my particular bottle naturally enough, knowing nothing about my little game; I poured my couple of fingers, and dropped it down as innocent as a lamb before I knew what I was doing. By George! my boy, 'twas like opening lock-gates; I was just heavenly gay before morning. There was one good thing about it, though—I never told Emily I was going to swear off; I was going to surprise her, so I had the disappointment all to myself. Maybe she isn't as happy as your wife; but, whatever else I've done, or not done, I've never lied to her."

"It's a pity you hadn't promised *her* then, before you tried your experiment," said Fred. The captain shook his head gravely and replied,

"I guess not; why, I'd have either killed somebody or killed myself if I'd gone on a day or two longer. I s'pose I'd have got along better if I'd had anybody to keep me company, or reason with me like a schoolmaster; but I hadn't; I didn't know anybody that I dared trust with a secret like that."

"*I* hadn't reformed then, eh?" queried Fred.

"You? why you're one of the very fellows I dodged! Just as I got aboard the boat—I came down late, on purpose—I saw you out aft. I tell you, I was under my blankets, with a towel wrapped around my jaw, in about one minute, and was just *a-praying* that you hadn't seen me come aboard."

Fred laughed, but his laughter soon made place for a look of tender solicitude. The unexpected turn that had been reached in the conversation he had so dreaded, and the sympathy which had been awakened in him by Crayme's confidence and openness, temporarily made of Fred Macdonald a man with whom Fred himself had never before been acquainted. A sudden idea struck him.

"Sam," said he, "try it over again, and *I'll* stay by you. I'll nurse you, crack jokes, fight off the blues for you, keep your friends away. I'll even break your neck for you, if you like, seeing it's you if it'll keep you straight."

"Will you, though?" said the captain, with a look of admiration undisguised, except by wonder. "You're the first friend I ever had, then. By thunder! how marrying Ettie Wedgewell *did* improve you, Fred! But," and the captain's face lengthened again, "there's a fellow's reputation to be considered, and where'll mine be after it gets around that I've sworn off?"

"Reputation be hanged!" exclaimed Fred. "*Lose* it, for your wife's sake. Besides, you'll *make* reputation instead of lose it: you'll be as famous as the Red River Raft, or the Mammoth Cave—the only thing of the kind west of the Alleghanies. As for the boys, tell them I've bet you a hundred that you can't stay off your liquor for a year, and that you're not the man to take a dare."

"*That* sounds like business," exclaimed the captain, springing to his feet.

"Let me draw up a pledge," said Fred eagerly, drawing pen and ink toward him.

"No, you don't, my boy," said the captain gently, and pushing Fred out of the room and upon the guards. "Emily shall do that. Below there!— Perkins, I've got to go up town for an hour; see if you can't pick up freight to pay laying-up expenses somehow. Fred, go home and get your traps; 'now's the accepted time,' as your father-in-law has dinged at me, many a Sunday, from the pulpit."

CHAPTER XIV.

A S Sam Crayme strode toward the body of the town, his business instincts took strong hold of his sentiments, in the manner natural alike to saints and sinners, and he laid a plan of operations against whiskey which was characterized by the apparent recklessness but actual prudence which makes for glory in steamboat captains, as it does in army commanders. As was his custom in business, he first drove at full speed upon the greatest obstacles ; so it came to pass that he burst into his own house, threw his arm around his wife with more than ordinary tenderness, and then looking into her eyes with the daring born of utter desperation, said,

" Emily, I came back to sign the strongest temperance pledge that you can possibly draw up; Fred Macdonald wanted to write out one, but I told him that nobody but you should do it ; you've earned the right to, poor girl." No such duty and surprise having ever before come hand in hand to

Mrs. Crayme, she acted as every true woman will imagine that she herself would have done under similar circumstances, and this action made it not so easy as it might otherwise have been to see just where the pen and ink were, or to prevent the precious document, when completed, from being disfigured by peculiar blots which were neither fingermarks nor ink-spots, yet which in shape and size suggested both of these indications of unneatness. Mrs. Crayme was not an adept at literary composition, and, being conscious of her own deficiencies, she begged that a verbal pledge might be substituted ; but her husband was firm.

"A contract don't steer worth a cent unless it's in writing, Emily," said he, looking over his wife's shoulder as she wrote. "Gracious, girl, you're making it too thin ; *any* greenhorn could sail right through that and all around it. Here, let *me* have it." And Crayme wrote, dictating aloud to himself as he did so, "And the—party—of the first part—hereby agrees to—do everything—else that the—spirit of this—agreement—seems to the party —of the second—part to—indicate or—imply." This he read over to his wife, saying,

"That's the way we fix contracts that aren't shipshape, Emily ; a steamboat couldn't be run in any other way." Then Crayme wrote at the foot of the paper, "Sam. Crayme, Capt. Str. *Excellence*," sur.. veyed the document with evident pride, and handed it to his wife, saying,

"Now, you see, you've got me so I can't ever get out of it by trying to make out that 'twas some other Sam Crayme that you reformed."

"O husband!" said Mrs. Crayme, throwing her arms about the captain's neck, "*don't* talk in that dreadful business way! I'm too happy to bear it. I want to go with you on this trip."

The captain shrank away from his wife's arms, and a cold perspiration started all over him as he exclaimed,

"Oh, don't, little girl! Wait till next trip. There's an unpleasant set of passengers aboard ; the barometer points to rainy weather, so you'd have to stay in the cabin all the time ; our cook is sick, and his cubs serve up the most infernal messes ; we're light of freight, and have got to stop at every warehouse on the river, and the old boat'll be either shrieking, or bumping, or blowing off steam the whole continual time."

Mrs. Crayme's happiness had been frightening

some of her years away, and her smile carried Sam himself back to his pre-marital period as she said,

"Never mind the rest ; I see you don't want me to go," and then she became Mrs. Crayme again as she said, pressing her face closely to her husband's breast, "but I hope you won't get *any* freight, *anywhere*, so you can get home all the sooner."

Then the captain called on Dr. White, and announced such a collection of symptoms that the doctor grew alarmed, insisted on absolute quiet, conveyed Crayme in his own carriage to the boat, saw him into his berth, and gave to Fred Macdonald a multitude of directions and cautions, the sober recording of which upon paper was of great service in saving Fred from suffering over the Quixotic aspect which the whole project had begun, in his mind, to take on. He felt ashamed even to look squarely into Crayme's eye, and his mind was greatly relieved when the captain turned his face to the wall and exclaimed,

"Fred, for goodness' sake get out of here ; I feel enough like a baby now, without having a nurse alongside. I'll do well enough for a few hours; just look in once in a while."

During the first day of the trip, Crayme made no

trouble for himself or Fred: under the friendly
shelter of night, the two men had a two-hour chat
which was alternately humorous, business-like, and
retrospective, and then Crayme fell asleep. The
next day was reasonably pleasant out of doors, so
the captain wrapped himself in a blanket and sat in
an extension-chair on the guards, where with solemn
face he received some condolences which went far to
keep him in good humor after the sympathizers had
departed. On the second night the captain was
restless, and the two men played cards. On the
third day the captain's physique reached the bottom of its stock of patience, and protested indig-
nantly at the withdrawal of its customary stimulus ; and it acted with more consistency, though
no less ugliness, than the human mind does when
under excitement and destitute of control. The
captain grew terribly despondent, and Fred found
ample use for all the good stories he knew. Some
of these amused the captain greatly, but after one
of them he sighed,

" Poor old Billy Hockess told me that the only
time I ever heard it before, and *didn't* we. have a
glorious time that night! He'd just put all his
money into the *Yenesei*—that blew up and took him

with it only a year afterward—and he gave us a new
kind of punch he'd got the hang of when he went
East for the boat's carpets. 'Twas made of two
bottles of brandy, one whiskey, two rum, one gin,
two sherry, and four claret, with guava jelly, and
lemon peel that had been soaking in curaçoa and
honey for a month. It looks kind of weak when
you think about it, but there were only six of us in
the party, and it went to the spot by the time we
got through. Golly, but didn't we make Rome howl
that night!"

Fred shuddered, and experimented upon his friend
with song; he was rewarded by hearing the captain hum an occasional accompaniment; but, as Fred
got fairly into a merry Irish song about one Terry
O'Rann, and uttered the lines in which the poet
states that the hero

> " —took whiskey punch
> Ivery night for his lunch,"

the captain put such a world of expression into
a long-drawn sigh that Fred began to feel depressed
himself; besides, songs were not numerous in Fred's
repertoire, and those in which there was no allu-
sion to drinking could be counted on half his fingers. Then he borrowed the bar-keeper's violin, and

3*

played, one after another, the airs which had been
his favorites in the days of his courtship, until
Crayme exclaimed,

"Say, Fred, we're not playing church ; give us
something that don't bring all of a fellow s dead
friends along with it."

Fred reddened, swung his bow viciously, and
dashed into " Natchez Under the Hill," an old air
which would have delighted Offenbach, but which
will never appear in a collection of classical music.

"Ah! that's something like music," exclaimed
Captain Crayme, as Fred paused suddenly to repair
a broken string.   " I never hear that but I think of
Wesley Treepoke, that used to run the *Quitman;*
went afterward to the *Rising Planet*, when the
Quitman's owners put her on a new line as an
opposition boat. Wess and I used to work things
so as to make Louisville at the same time—he going
up, I going down, and then turn about—and we
always had a glorious night of it, with one or two
other lively boys that we'd pick up. And Wess had
a fireman that could fiddle off old ' Natchez ' in a
way that would just make a corpse dance till its
teeth rattled, and that fireman would always be
called in just as we'd got to the place where you

can't tell what sort of whiskey 'tis you're drinking, and I tell you, 'twas so heavenly that a fellow could forgive the last boat that beat him on the river, or stole a landing from him. And *such* whiskey as Wess kept! used to go cruising around the back country, sampling little lots run out of private stills. He'd always find nectar, you'd better believe. Poor old boy! the tremens took him off at last. He hove his pilot overboard just before he died, and put a bullet into Pete Langston, his second clerk—they were both trying to hold him, you see—but they never laid it up against him. I wish I knew what became of the whiskey he had on hand when he walked off—no, I don't, either; what am I thinking about? But I do, though—hanged if I don't!"

Fred grew pale: he had heard of drunkards growing delirious upon ceasing to drink; he had heard of men who, in periods of aberration, were impelled by the motive of the last act or recollection which strongly impressed them; what if the captain should suddenly become delirious, and try to throw *him* overboard or shoot him? Fred determined to get the captain at once upon the guards—no, into the cabin, where there would be no sight of water to suggest anything dreadful—and search his room for pistols. But the captain objected to being moved into the cabin.

"The boys," said the captain, alluding to the gamblers, "are mighty sharp in the eye, and like as not they'd see through my little game, and then where'd my reputation be? Speaking of the boys reminds me of Harry Genang, that cleaned out that rich Kentucky planter at bluff one night, and then swore off gambling for life and gave a good-by supper aboard the boat. 'Twas just at the time when Prince Imperial Champagne came out, and the whole supper was made of that splendid stuff. I guess I must have put away four bottles, and if I'd known how much he'd ordered, I could have carried away a couple more. I've always been sorry I didn't."

Fred wondered if there was any subject of conversation which would not suggest liquor to the captain; he even brought himself to ask if Crayme had seen the new Methodist Church at Barton since it had been finished.

"Oh, yes," said the captain; " I started to walk Moshier home one night, after we'd punished a couple of bottles of old Crow whiskey at our house, and he caved in all of a sudden, and I laid him out on the steps of that very church till I could get a carriage. Those were my last two bottles of Crow, too; it's too bad the way the good things of this life paddle off."

The captain raised himself in his berth, sat on the edge thereof, stood up, stared out the window, and began to pace his room with his head down and his hands behind his back. Little by little he raised his head, dropped his hands, flung himself into a chair, beat the devil's tattoo on the table, sprang up excitedly, and exclaimed,

"I'm going back on all the good times I ever had."

"You're only getting ready to try a new kind, Sam," said Fred.

"Well, I'm going back on my friends."

"Not on all of them; the dead ones would pat you on the back, if they got a chance."

"A world without whiskey looks infernally dismal to a fellow that isn't half done living."

"It looks first-rate to a fellow that hasn't got any back-down in him."

"Curse you! I wish I'd made *you* back down when you first talked temperance to me."

"Go ahead! Then curse your wife—don't be afraid; you've been doing it ever since you married her."   ·

Crayme flew at Macdonald's throat; the younger man grappled the captain and threw him into his bunk. The captain struggled and glared like a tiger; Fred gasped, between the special efforts dictated by self-preservation,

"Sam, I—promised to—to see you—through—and I'm—going to—do it, if—if I have to—break your neck."

The captain made one tremendous effort; Fred braced one foot against the table, put a knee on the captain's breast, held both the captain's wrists tightly, looked full into the captain's eyes, and breathed a small prayer—for his own safety. For a moment or two, perhaps longer, the captain strained violently, and then relaxed all effort and cried,

"Fred, you've whipped me!"

"Nonsense! whip yourself," exclaimed Fred, "if you're going to stop drinking."

The captain turned his face to the wall and said nothing; but he seemed to be so persistently swallowing something that Fred suspected a secreted

bottle, and moved an investigation so suddenly
that the captain had not time in which to wipe his
eyes.

" Hang it, Fred," said he, rather brokenly; " how
can what's babyish in men whip a full-grown steamboat captain ? "

" The same way that it whipped a full-grown
woolen-mill manager once, I suppose, old boy," said
Macdonald.

" Is that so ? " exclaimed the captain, astonishment getting so sudden an advantage over shame
that he turned over and looked his companion in
the face. " Why—how are you, Fred ? I feel as if
I was just being introduced. Didn't anybody else
help ? "

" Yes," said Fred, " a woman ; but—you've got a
wife, too."

Crayme fell back on his pillow and sighed. " If
I could only *think* about her, Fred ! But I can't ;
whiskey's the only thing that comes into my
mind."

"Can't think about her ! " exclaimed Fred; "why,
are you acquainted with her yet, I wonder ? *I'll*
never forget the evening you were married."

" That *was* jolly, wasn't it ? " said Crayme. " I'll

bet such sherry was never opened west of the Alleghanies, before or —"

"*Hang* your sherry!" roared Fred; "it's your wife that I remember. *You* couldn't see her, of course, for you were standing alongside of her; but the rest of us—well, I wished myself in your place, that's all."

"Did you, though?" said Crayme, with a smile which seemed rather proud; "well, I guess old Major Pike did too, for he drank to her about twenty times that evening. Let's see; she wore a white moire antique, I think they called it, and it cost twenty-one dollars a dozen, and there was at least one broken bottle in every —"

"And I made up my mind she was throwing herself away, in marrying a fellow that would be sure to care more for whiskey than he did for her," interrupted Fred.

"Ease off, Fred, ease off now; there wasn't any whiskey there; I tried to get some of the old Twin Tulip brand for punch, but — "

"But the devil happened to be asleep, and you got a chance to behave yourself," said Fred.

Crayme looked appealingly. "Fred," said he, ' tell me about her yourself; I'll take it as a favor."

"Why, she looked like a lot of lilies and roses," said Fred, "except that you couldn't tell where one left off and the other began. As she came into the room *I* felt like getting down on my knees. Old Bayle was telling me a vile story just then, but the minute *she* came in he stopped as if he was shot."

"He wouldn't drink a drop that evening," said Crayme, "and I've puzzled my wits over that for five years ——"

"She looked *so* proud of *you*," interrupted Fred with some impatience.

"Did she?" asked Crayme. "Well, I guess I *was* a good-looking fellow in those days: I know Pike came up to me once, with a glass in his hand, and said that he ought to drink to *me*, for I was the finest-looking groom he'd ever seen. He was so tight, though, that he couldn't hold his glass steady; and though you know I never had a drop of stingy blood in me, it *did* go to my heart to see him spill that gorgeous sherry."

"She looked very proud of *you*," Fred repeated; "but I can't see why, for I've never seen her do it since."

"You *will*, though, hang you!" exclaimed the

captain. " Get out of here! I can think about her *now*, and I don't want anybody else around. No rudeness meant, you know, Fred."

Fred Macdonald retired quietly, taking with him the keys of both doors, and feeling more exhausted than he had been on any Saturday night since the building of the mill.

CHAPTER XV.

A FIRST INWARD PEEP.

AMONG the Barton people who had actually made any effort for the sake of temperance, no one found greater comfort in contemplative retrospects of his own work than Deacon Jones. True, his contributions to the various funds which Crupp, Tomple, Wedgewell, and Brown devised had not been as great as had been expected of him; nor had such moneys as he finally gave been obtained from him without an amount of effort which Crupp declared sufficient to effect the extraction, from the soil, of the stump of a centenarian oak; but when the money had left his pocket, and was absolutely beyond recall, the deacon made the most he could out of it by the only method which remained. His contributions gave him an excuse for talk and exhortation, and, next to money-making, there was no operation which the deacon enjoyed as much as that of exhorting others to good deeds. Until there broke out in Barton the temperance excitement alluded to in our first chapter, Deacon Jones's hortatory efforts had been principally of a religious nature; he believed in religion, and he occasionally extracted enjoyment from it; besides, his thrifty soul had always been profoundly moved by the business-like nature of the Scripture passage, "Whoso shall convert a sinner from the error of his ways, shall save a soul from death and cover a multitude of sins." Many had been the unregenerate in Barton with whom the deacon had labored, generally with considerable tact, as to occasion and language, and sometimes with success. His orthodoxy was acceptable to every pastor in the village, for he was an extreme believer in every religious tenet which either pastor declared necessary to salvation; and his frequent inability to reconcile such of these ideas as conflicted with each other only led the ministers to accord new admiration to a faith which was appalled by nothing. Up to the time when he took active part in the temperance movement, one of his favorite injunctions had been, "Lay up your treasure in heaven;" when, however, he found himself suddenly and frequently called upon for contributions, he dropped this injunction in favor of that one which reads, "Give to him that ask-

eth of thee." It had been a matter of considerable sorrow to the deacon that his first knowledge
of this passage had been derived from St. Luke
instead of St. Matthew, and that he had many times
been compelled to say " Give to *every man*," etc.,
which quotation had reacted upon him in a manner
which caused him to quote to himself, " Many are
the afflictions of the righteous," and to suffer some
terrible flounderings in the twin pits of logic and
casuistry; but when he corrected himself according
to Matthew, his heart was gladdened, and his restraint removed. The old man talked a great deal
out of honest delight in righteousness and humanity; but he was never moved to reticence by the
thought that if his scattered seed produced a fair
share of grain, the demands upon his own precious
store would be lessened.

Besides, the deacon could, with propriety, urge a
more conspicuous form of well-doing than mere
contributions of currency ever attained to. Had
not he himself taken upon his shoulders Tom
Adams, driver of the brick-yard team? If any one
doubted it, or had never been made acquainted
with the fact, the deacon gave him no excuse for
farther ignorance. One after another of the well-

to-do merchants, professional men, and farmers, were
urged by the deacon to take entire charge of some
unfortunate soul, after the manner of the deacon
himself with Tom, and to all of these he insisted
that what he had done for Tom he had been richly
paid for by the approving smiles of his own conscience. Shrewd judges of human nature were convinced that if such payment was made to the deacon,
he was doubly paid, for Tom Adams had been a
treasure of a workman ever since he had stopped
drinking; but, with the marvelous blindness of the
man who objects to seeing, the deacon clearly com-
prehended both aspects of the situation, without
ever once allowing them to interfere with each other.

He was pursuing his favorite line of argument in
his store one afternoon, before Parson Brown, Lawyer Bottom, the postmaster, Dr. White, and two or
three others who were not active customers at that
immediate moment, and, as all his hearers but the
parson were in good circumstances, the deacon felt
called upon to make an unusual effort.

" Tell you what it is, gentlemen," said he, " there's
nothin' like puttin' your hand in your pocket to
show you what doin' good is. Here I've been
thinkin' all my life that I was doin' good by sub-

scribin' to Bible Societies, Missionary Societies, an' all such things, and yet there was *the* chance right in my own hands, and I was too blind to see it. I done it at last on a risk, as if God didn't know best when he inspires men to righteous deeds; an' I was fearful, time an' again, that it mightn't turn out well; but I've been more abundantly blessed at it than I ever expected to be. It makes a man feel kind of like Christ must have felt, to be able to help a fellow-creature out of his troubles and sins. Look at Tom Adams now! he's always sober, his children go to Sunday-school, and he's never around looking as if you'd rather not meet him, and *I*, thank the Lord! feel even better over it than *he* does."

The postmaster slyly tipped a grave wink at Lawyer Bottom, and the lawyer sagely laid a wise forefinger athwart his own nose. Dr. White dropped a short bark, intended for a cough, which somehow provoked a smile all around. Suddenly a small boy rushed into the store, exclaiming,

"O Deacon Jones! Tom Adams fell out of the wagon and broke his leg!"

The deacon's ecstatic expression instantly vanished into thin air, and he asked, with a face full of misery,

"And the horses ran away?"

"No," said the boy. "*They're* all right."

Dr. White sprang up, seized his cane, and asked, "Where is he?"

"That's so," asked the deacon, still more sorrowful of countenance, as he continued, "just as corn's beginnin' to come in, too, an' needin' to be measured an' sacked; that's just the way things go in this wicked world!"

Lawyer Bottom, who did not believe much in God, and believed still less in the deacon, asked,

"Well, deacon, then you wouldn't advise me to take somebody on my hands for the sake of the spiritual payment I'll be likely to get out of the operation?"

The deacon rallied himself by a tremendous effort, but his countenance did not indicate that the answer he was about to make would be of that softness that turns away wrath; he was saved from disgracing himself, however, by still another boy, who came flying through the main street on horseback, shouting,

"Fire! fire! The woolen mill! Fire!"

The deacon's store emptied in an instant of every one but Parson Brown, for all the other listeners were men of some means, and stockholders in the mill.

"Here!" shouted the deacon, cutting the cords of a "nest" of pails; "take buckets along with you; like enough it'll need everybody's help, and the mill's only half insured, too! Parson, would you mind sittin' here until my boy gets back? I'm losin' enough to-day without having to shut up store, too."

"Certainly, I'll stay," said the old preacher, limping to the front of the store, and laying his hand on the shoulder of the troubled store-keeper; "but, Brother Jones, if the light of that burning mill should show you anything inside of yourself, *don't* cover your eyes. It's for righteousness' sake I ask it."

"All right, Brother Brown," whispered the deacon hoarsely, as he started off with two water-pails in each hand, and murmuring, "What did the old fellow mean by that, I wonder?" Across the street was Squire Tomple, just jumping into his buggy, and the deacon made haste to accept an invitation to a seat beside his fellow-sufferer. The two stockholders did not lack company; Crupp, Judge Macdonald, and most of the other stockholders, either preceded or followed them, and on the road were hundreds of men and boys, full of an enterprising desire to see the largest fire that had ever occurred in Barton, and already experiencing such of the pleasures of anticipation as a heavy column of smoke could create. Coming in sight of the mill itself, the deacon groaned, and the Squire assisted him, for flames were bursting from every window, and the men who had been passing pails of water up ladders and through the stairways had been driven from their work, and had formed a circle which was slowly but steadily widening. Considerable of the wool had been removed and stacked outside the building, and it now became necessary to move this still farther away, but so many hands were ready to seize it that Deacon Jones could not relieve his feelings even by attempting to save property ; so he stood still and looked at the fire, as he estimated his losses. Such a day he had not known since he had lost considerable uninsured stock by the explosion of a river steamer. Sidling uneasily about among the crowd, he found several stockholders anxiously comparing pencil notes, and the figures were anything but consolatory ; supposing all the stock to be saved, there was yet the mill

and machinery—value, about ten thousand dollars
—which would be totally lost ; insurance, five thousand dollars ; dead loss, ditto ; which left the Squire
out of pocket to the extent of a quarter of his
subscription. The small profit which had already
accrued would not more than cover the loss of the
interest on the remaining capital until the mill
could be rebuilt, if it seemed advisable to rebuild it.

"Who's to blame for all this?" asked the deacon
angrily.

" We haven't learned yet," said the judge, " and
I'm afraid it won't help matters any to know all
about it. There goes the last of it ! "

As the judge spoke, the blazing frame fell, the
small boys shouted " Oh——h ! " in chorus, and the
deacon's heart sank like lead as he turned away.
He had lost, say, a hundred and fifty dollars by the
fire, and Tom Adams's misfortune would entail additional loss upon him, for a new man would have to
be watched and taught and helped, whereas Tom
worked as easily as the wheel of a machine. It was
but right that the deacon should regret his losses ;
for though he was a man of considerable property,
a dollar looked very large to him, for the reason that
his first dollars had each one represented an enor-

8

mous amount of labor.   But when Lawyer Bottom,
who had invested in mill stock only with the hope
of profit, approached the deacon, and asked, with
more curiosity than malice, " How about temperance now, deacon ? " the facial contortions which
the deacon offered in reply sent the lawyer away in
an ecstasy of unholy glee, which almost eradicated
his own sense of loss, and which dispelled for a time
such little belief as he had in the transforming
power of religion.   But what is one man's poison is
another's food.   The lawyer's question was not entirely disposed of by the deacon's ungracious reply ;
it repeated itself time and again to the old man,
and at the most inopportune times and places ;
it came to him behind the counter, and made him
give wrong weights and measures, with the bal-
ance not always in his favor ; it came to him when
he was making entries in his day-book, and caused
him to forget certain items ; at his own dinner-table
it suddenly made itself heard, and interfered with his
relish of the good viands which he so much enjoyed ;
it dropped in upon him in his dreams, when he
could not be on his guard against his better self,
and extracted from his conscience a provoking line
of answers which in his waking hours he could not

gainsay. For three days this depressing experience continued, and then there occurred, at the regular weekly prayer-meeting of Parson Wedgewell's church, an episode which for months caused mournful reflections in the minds of such of Parson Wedgewell's parishioners as were not in the habit of attending prayer-meeting. It was noticed by the faithful that Deacon Jones looked unusually solemn and sensitive as he entered the room, and that he did not, as had been hitherto his habit, start the second hymn. This omission having been made good by some enterprising member, however, the deacon got upon his feet and said:

"Brethren, during the past few days my eyes have been opened, and what I have seen hasn't been pleasant to look upon. It is indeed true, my dear friends, that Satan sometimes appears as an angel of light. For months I've been feeling, and real happily, too, what a glorious thing it was to do good; I had been instrumental in saving one man from destruction by keeping him busy, and I'd helped save another"—here the deacon paused suddenly and looked around to make sure that Judge Macdonald was not in the room—"I'd helped save another by taking an interest in the mill. But

within a few days I've learned that my own righteousness was as filthy rags ; 'twas even worse than
that, brethren, for the worst rags are worth so much
a pound, but I can't find that my righteousness is
worth anything at all. I've fought it out with myself, brethren, an' I believe I've conquered ; but it
makes my heart sick to see what my enemy looks
like, an' to think I've got to carry him around with
me through the rest of my days. Doin' good's all
right, even if it *does* pay in dollars and cents, brethren ; but doin' good for the sake of what it'll bring
is the quickest way of makin' a hypocrite that I ever
found, an' I'm beginnin' to think that I've found
a good many ways in myself, my friends. I ask an
interest in the prayers of God's people, an' I assure
'em that there's no danger of any of their prayers
bein' wasted."

The deacon dropped into his seat, and the silence
that prevailed for a moment was simply inevitable
in a little company that had never before heard
such an extraordinary confession ; as one of the
members afterward remarked, it sounded like a
murderer's last dying speech. Then good Parson
Wedgewell sprang to his feet, and, with streaming
eyes and rapid utterances, offered a prayer such as

had never been heard in that room before. The songs and prayers which followed were not those to which the meeting were accustomed, and when at last the assemblage separated, there could not be heard from the home-wending couples any critiques of the language or garb of any one who had been present.

As for Deacon Jones, he continued his new fight most valiantly by visiting Tom Adams that very evening, and assuring him that, their supplementary agreement to the contrary notwithstanding, he would continue Tom's pay during his confinement, and would pay his doctor's bill also.

CHAPTER XVI.

DURING the day or two which followed his interview with Tappelmine, Father Baguss was consumed with conflicting emotions. He could not deny that his offer to help Tappelmine had taken an unpleasant load off of his own heart; but it was equally certain that the contemplation of the possible results of the arrangement gave him a sense of oppression, which differed from the first in quality, but of which the quantity was far too great to be endured with comfort. To find a way of getting out of the whole matter was a suggestion which came frequently to the heart of the old man, and was not as rigidly excluded as it would have been from that of the reader; but fortunately for the honesty of Father Baguss, his ingenuity was of the lowest order conceivable; so he did as thousands of his betters have done when unable, by any abandonment of self-respect, to avoid the inevitable: he submitted, and groaned frequently to the Lord. Some-

times these efforts before the Unseen increased the
old man's lugubriousness; at other times, a song
came to his rescue, followed by a troop of its own
kind; but so uncertain were his moods that Mrs.
Baguss, who never before had occasion to suppose
that there was a single nerve in her husband's body,
began to complain that she didn't "believe in this
thing of lookin' out for other folks, if it makes you
cranky with your own."

The old man's trouble increased on the third day,
for Tappelmine dropped in and hinted vaguely that
it was not yet too late to plant winter wheat. The
old man went into Tappelmine's field with his own
team, and plowed; he worked his horses longer
hours than he ever did on his own ground; he lent
an extra horse to work with Tappelmine's own before a harrow; he himself sowed the wheat, casting
now plentifully, as he thought of what Tappelmine
might owe him by harvest-time, and now scantily,
as he thought of what might be his own fate if the
crop should be troubled with rust, or blight, or rain,
or drought. And all the while, as he followed his
horses, the old man kept uttering short petitions
for Tappelmine and himself; and all the while his
soul was full of unspoken prayers for heavy rains or

sudden cold, so that the work might be stopped by
the hand of Providence himself. But no such for-
tune befell the good old man: such an open fall had
not been known since the settlement of Barton;
even the Indian summer lasted so long that the
poet of the Barton *Register* found opportunity to
publish, in three successive weekly numbers, "odes,"
which could be read in the weather which suggested them. When a heavy rain at last put an
end to field work, there were twenty-seven acres
in wheat on the Tappelmine estate. Father Baguss
ached in soul and body, but the wheat-field work
was but the beginning of sorrow. The Tappelmine
larder was bareness itself; there was not a porker
in the Tappelmine pen; there was not even corn
enough in the Tappelmine crib to feed the family
horse, let alone to send to mill, and be ground into
the meal which the Tappelmines fortunately preferred to fine flour. Father Baguss sold the necessities of life in small quantities to his neighbor,
with the understanding that they were to be repaid
by the labor of Tappelmine, who was to get out material for barrel-staves and wheelwright's spokes on
the old man's woodland; but, by the time the wheat
was planted, Tappelmine, who, under the eye of

Baguss, did more work in a month than he had done in the whole of the year which preceded, and who during the month had been pretty effectually kept from his accustomed stimulant, fell sick. Then the cup of misery which Father Baguss had put to his own lips was full; as the old man, in his homely way, explained to his own pastor, it didn't run over, and that was just the trouble; he had to drink it all. He sought for sympathy among his neighbors and acquaintances, but without much success; the Barton postmaster expressed the sentiment of the township, when he said that " no one but a thick-headed blunderer like Baguss would attempt to reform a dead-and-gone soaker like Tappelmine." Besides, most of the inhabitants wanted to see how the case was going to turn out, and all of them instinctively understood that the best point of view is always at a respectable distance from the object to be looked at. The sorrowing philanthropist went to Crupp, Tomple, and Deacon Jones; but these three reformers, knowing that Baguss could afford the loss, quietly agreed with each other that it would be indeed consolatory to have a companion in experience; so they made excuses, and quoted figures in evidence, and Father Baguss went home with the settled conviction that he would have to look to Providence for his only assistance.

But while Providence was thus reforming Father Baguss, Tappelmine was growing steadily weaker, and Baguss found his causes of discomfort increased by a debate, which lasted long in his mind, whether it might not be better, for the sake of the drunkard's family, to let Tappelmine die, and then lease the farm himself at a price which would support the widow. While one phase of the case was present in his mind, he would suggest to the doctor that medicine didn't seem to do any good—which was certainly true—and that he didn't believe it would pay to come so often ; when, on the contrary, conscience would argue for its own side, the old man would have all three of the physicians visit Tappelmine in rapid succession. The doctors disagreed, as any one but Father Baguss would have known. Perry suggested electrical treatment, which would necessitate the purchase of a battery, no such piece of mechanism having ever been seen in the town except in a locked cabinet of the Barton High School. Dr. White outlined a course of treatment which seemed reasonable to Father Baguss, but which, put into practice, did neither good nor harm ;

while Pykem arranged for certain inexpensive ap-
plications of water, with results which were in the
main encouraging. But Tappelmine was unable to
leave his bed for three months, and when he was at
all fit to work, he could labor for but two or three
hours a day.

And so Father Baguss found himself brought
down to the position of a man who was spending
money without knowing what he was to get for it.
Such a position he had never occupied before, and
no one could wonder that he felt uncomfortable in
it ; but the duration of the period was such that the
victim succumbed to the steady pressure of truths
which, in their abstract form, would have been as
ineffective against him as against an acute logi-
cian whose intellect had been trained by his
pocket.

But Father Baguss was not the only instrument
of the salvation of Tappelmine. In existence, but
scarcely known of or recognized, there was a Mrs.
Tappelmine. With face, hair, eyes, and garments
of the same color, the color itself being neutral ;
small, thin, faded, inconspicuous, poorly clad, bent
with labors which had yielded no return, as dead to
the world as saints strive to be, yet remaining in

the world for the sake of those whom she had often
wished out of it, Mrs. Tappelmine devoted herself to the wreck of what was once a hope over
which her eyes had been of a luster which high-born
maidens had envied, and a hope in which her heart
had throbbed with a joy which had seemed too
great for life to hold. About the bedside of her
husband she hovered day and night. When she
slept no one but herself knew, and she herself did
not care. When Tappelmine made his verbal
agreement with Father Baguss, she had listened
with a joy whose earnestness was as nothing compared with her resolution. She had hurried away
from the broken window to a corner where her
dirty children were at quarrelsome play, and she
had bestowed upon each of them a passionate
caress which startled even the little wretches themselves into wondering silence. From that moment
she watched her husband's every movement, and
Tappelmine, like a true Pike—for the Pike, like the
Transcendentalist, existed ages before he found his
way into literature—Tappelmine subjected himself
into his wife's dominion. He made numberless excuses to go to some place where liquor could be
found ; she, with the wisdom of the serpent, yet the

gentleness of the dove, prevented him. As, through the course of her husband's labors, under the eye of Baguss, he had grown more silent than ever, she had increased her exertions for his comfort; when, finally, the task was completed, and Tappelmine, with thinner face and hollower eyes than ever, fell heavily upon his rude bed and uttered—almost screamed— the single word " Whiskey ! " she was on her knees beside him in an instant.

" Jerry," she exclaimed, "you've got the better of whiskey these late days."

" Just a drop more—to keep me from dying," gasped Tappelmine.

" Don't, Jerry," she pleaded. " Let me hold you tight, so you *can't* die."

" Just a drop, for God's sake, Mariar ! " said Tappelmine imploringly.

" O Jerry ! " replied the wife, " don't—for the children's sake; *they're* more to you than God is. I hope he'll forgive me for sayin' it."

" Only a single mouthful, Mariar," said Tappelmine, " to keep me from sinkin'."

"You're not sinkin', old man—Jerry, dear; you're gittin' *up*. *Keep* up, Jerry."

" I'll be all right in a day or two, Mariar, if I only

get a taste. You don't want a sick man a-layin' around, not fit to do for his young ones?"

"You don't need to, Jerry. *I'll* do for 'em, if you'll only—only make 'em proud of you."

"It'll make me good for more to *you*, old woman—one single mouthful will," said Tappelmine.

"You've been better to me these three weeks than you ever was before, Jerry; keep on bein' so, won't you? It puts me in mind of old times—times when you used to laugh, an' kiss me."

"I'd be that way again," said Tappelmine, "if I could only pick up stren'th."

"You're that way now, Jerry, if you only stay as you are."

"*You'll* die, Mariar," said the man, "if I don't get out of this bed some way—you an' the young uns."

"I'd be glad enough," said the woman, "if you'd only stay, Jerry."

"An' the boys an' girls?" queried Tappelmine.

"Would be better off alongside of me in the ground, rather than have their dad go backwards again," said Mrs. Tappelmine. "People turn up their noses at 'em now, Jerry."

" What are you drivin' at, Mariar ? "

" Why, Jerry, when the children go 'long the road
--God knows I don't let 'em do it oftener than I
can help—folks see 'em dirty, an' wearin' poor
clothes, an' not lookin' over an' above fed up, an' they
can't help kind o' twitchin' up their faces at 'em
once there was a time when I couldn't have helped
doin' it to young ones lookin' that way."

" *Curse* people ! " exclaimed Tappelmine.

" They do it to me, too," continued the woman.

Tappelmine sprang up, and exclaimed fiercely,

" What for ? "

" 'Cause—'cause you've made 'em, I reckon, Jerry,"
answered Mrs. Tappelmine with some difficulty, oc-
casioned by some choking sobs which nearly took
exclusive possession of her. " You know, Jerry, I
don't say it to complain—complainin' never seems to
bring one any good to a woman like me ; but—if
you only knowed how folks look at me in—in stores,
an' everywhere else, you—wouldn't blame me for
not likin' it. *I* didn't ever do anything to bring it
about, unless 'twas in marryin' *you*, and I *ain't* sorry
I did *that ;* but I wish I didn't ever have to
see anybody again, if you're goin' to keep on
drinkin'."

The sick man fell back and was silent; his wife threw herself beside him, crying,

" Don't get mad at me, Jerry; God knows it's the deadest truth."

After a moment or two Tappelmine laid a hand on his wife's cheek, where it had not been before for twenty years; once its touch had brought blushes; now, tears hurried down to meet it, and yet Mrs. Tappelmine was happier than when she had been a pretty Kentucky girl, twenty years before.

" Mariar," said Tappelmine at last, " I've dragged you all down."

" No, you haven't, Jerry," asserted Mrs. Tappelmine, with a lie which she could not avoid.

" If dyin'll help you up again, I'm willin'," continued Tappelmine.

The apartments in the Tappelmine mansion were so few that it was impossible for anything unusual to transpire without attracting the attention of all the inmates; so it followed that the children, beholding the actions of their parents, had gradually approached the bed with countenances whose blankness was painfully eloquent to the sick man. Tappelmine looked at them, and grew more miserable of visage; he hid his face beside his wife,

groaned " No more whiskey if I die for it ! " and
jumped up and kissed each of his children, while
Mrs. Tappelmine sobbed aloud, and Father Baguss,
who, coming over a few moments before to talk
business, had heard the simple word " whiskey," and
had since been jealously listening under the window, sneaked away muttering to himself,

"After all I've done for him, I can't even say to
myself that *I* saved him."

CHAPTER XVII.

THE CONCLUSION OF THE WHOLE MATTER

THE fire which destroyed the Mississippi Valley Woolen Mills did such damage in the ranks of the temperance reformers that for a few months Crupp, Tomple, and several others had frequent cause to feel lonesome, while poor Father Baguss fell back upon the church for that comfort which, just after his first effort with Tappelmine, and before the fire, he had frequently found in the society of his self-approving brother stockholders. The mill was rebuilt, only a few of the owners of stock refusing to be assessed for their proportion of the loss; the mill made a very prosperous winter, and interested persons were not averse to talking about it; but after Deacon Jones' speech was noised abroad, the mill was no longer a semi-holy topic of conversation, which was allowable even on the church steps on Sundays. Some of the men whose eyes had been opened toward themselves, on the occasion of the fire, were honest enough to confess to themselves, and to bring forth fruits meet for repentance ; but the majority took refuge either in open or secret sophistry, with the comforting impression that they blinded others as effectually as they did themselves. The mass of the people, however—those who neither subscribed to temperance funds, nor mill stock, nor anything else, still looked on, and were plethoric of encouragement and criticism. When appealed to for help, their logic was simply bewildering, and almost as depraved as the same defensive and offensive weapon is in politics. Tomple was the man to do such work, said some, for he was the rich man of the village, and rich men are only God's stewards ; others suggested Captain Crayme, who had money, and who should be willing to spend considerable of it as a thank-offering for his own providential deliverance from the thraldom of drink. The irreligious thought that all such work should be done by the church, if churches were good for anything but to shout in ; while the religious felt that the irreligious, among whom could be found nearly every drinker in the village, should expend whatever money was needed for the physical reformation of their kind. Where none of these excuses seemed available, or wherever two or three conservatives of differing views met

together, there was always Crupp to fall back upon ;
each man could grasp his own pocket-book with
tender tenacity, and declare to a sympathetic audience that the man who had coined his money out
of widows' tears and orphans' groans should by
rights take care of all the drunkards in the county,
even until he was so reduced in means as to be
dependent upon public charity for his own support.

Thus matters stood when a year had elapsed
since the memorable temperance meeting, and Parson Wedgewell suggested that an anniversary service would be only an ordinary and decent testimonial of respect to Providence for his special
mercies during the year.   To the parson's surprise,
Crupp who—though he had during the winter surprised every one by joining Parson Wedgewell's
church, in spite of a very severe course of ques-
tioning by the Examining Committee—was still a
man of action and a contemner of mere words—
Crupp not only failed to oppose such a meeting, but
volunteered himself to write for Major Ben Bailey,
the gifted orator who had addressed the earlier
meeting, and to pay the orator's expenses. Such
offers were rarely made, even by the Barton reformers, so by unanimous consent Crupp wrote to the

great lecturer, it being admitted by Tomple, Wedgewell, Baguss, and Jones, that Crupp's idea of informing the Major what had been done during the
year was a good one, and that it would enable the
orator to modify his address with special reference
to existing circumstances. But Squire Tomple and
the parson were considerably astonished to see
Crupp dash into the Squire's store one day, exhibiting an unusual degree of excitement, as he un-
folded a letter and remarked,

"He won't come! Just listen to what he says!"
And while the two other reformers stood as if they
saw the sky falling and did not despair of catching
it in their eyes and mouths, Crupp read:

"In replying to Mr. Crupp's favor of the —th,
Major Bailey can only say, that while he should be
glad to again meet the people among whom so
great an amount of good has been accomplished
within the year, he cannot see that he can render
any service. Major Bailey's efforts are confined
solely to the awakening of an interest in temperance ; the condition of affairs which Mr. Crupp reports as existing in Barton, however, indicates a
degree of interest which cannot be heightened by
any effort which the writer could put forth. What

seems desirable at Barton is such an informing of the general populace upon what has been accomplished, upon the manner in which the work has been done, and the comparatively small number of persons who have actively participated in it, as shall convince the inhabitants that they did not fulfill their whole duty toward temperance when a year ago they applauded the utterances of the writer of these lines. Briefly, Major Bailey feels that if he attended, he could contribute only such efforts as, under the circumstances, would be entirely out of place."

"Astonishing!" exclaimed Parson Wedgewell, with the eye of a man who dreams.

"Threw away a job!" said Tomple, like the thrifty business man that he was.

But the meeting was planned and widely advertised, and when, on the evening appointed, the attendants looked over the room, they found occasion for considerable attentive reflection.

Except that Major Ben Bailey, the gifted orator, was not present, the meeting presented the same attractions which had drawn such a crowd to its predecessor. The Barton Brass Band was there, and with some new airs learned during the year; the Crystal Spring Glee Club was there ; there were the pastors of the four churches in Barton, and Squire Tomple was in the chair as before. Besides, there were additional attractions: Crupp, a year before, the man who was lending to liquor selling an air of respectability, was upon the platform to the left and rear of Squire Tomple; old Bunley, who a year before had been responsible only as a container of alcohol, but now a respectable citizen and book-keeper to Squire Tomple, occupied the secretary's chair; Tom Adams acted as usher in one of the side-aisles, and dragged all the heavy drinkers up to front seats; Harry Wainright was there, with a wife whose vail was not thick enough to hide her happiness; Fred Macdonald, who had spent the evening of the other meeting in the Barton House bar-room, was there; so was Tappelmine, appearing as ill at ease as a porker in a strange field, but still there; while in a side seat, close to the wall, sitting as much in the shadow of his wife as possible, so as to guard his professional reputation, was Sam Crayme, captain of the steamer *Excellence*. A number of "the boys" were there also, and yet the church was not only not crowded, but not even full. During the year temperance had been guided from the hearts to the pockets of a great many,

and this radical treatment had been fatal to many
an enthusiastic soul that had theretofore been
blameless in its own eyes. Those who attended
heard some music, however, which was not de-
ficient in point of quality; they heard a short but live
address from old Parson Fish on the moral beauty
of a temperate life, and an earnest prayer from that
one of the Barton pastors who had during the year
done nothing which justified the mention of his
name in this history, and then the audience saw
Mr. Crupp advance to the front of the platform
and unfold a large sheet of paper, which he crum-
pled in one hand as he spoke as follows :

" Ladies and gentlemen : having been requested,
by the chairman of the last meeting, to collect some
statistics of the work accomplished in Barton, during the past year, in the cause of temperance, I in-
vite your attention to the following figures :

" Population of township last year, three thousand two hundred and sixty-five. Signatures to
pledge, at last meeting, six hundred and twenty-
seven [applause]; signatures of persons who were in
the habit of drinking at time of signing, two hundred and thirty-one ; number of persons who have
broken the pledge since signing, one hundred and

sixty [sighs and groans]; number of persons who
have kept their pledges, seventy-one [applause];
number reclaimed by personal effort since meeting,
forty-six [applause]; amount of money subscribed
and applied strictly for the good of the cause, and
without hope of pecuniary gain [a faint hiss or two],
five thousand one hundred and ninety dollars and
thirty-eight cents [tremendous applause]; amount
which has been returned by the beneficiaries without
solicitation, twenty-seven dollars [laughter, hisses,
and groans]. Of the amount subscribed, *six-sevenths*
came from *five* persons, who own less than *one-fif-
tieth* part of the taxable property of the township."

The quiet which prevailed, as Mr. Crupp spoke
these last words and took his seat, was, if considered
only *as* quiet, simply faultless ; but its duration was
greater and more annoying than things purely faultless usually are, and there was a general sensation
of relief when Squire Tomple, who during the year
had not made any public display of his charities,
and who was popularly supposed to care as much
for a dollar as any one, slowly got upon his feet

" My friends," said the Squire, " I'm more than
ever convinced that temperance is a good thing
[hearty applause], and the reason I feel so is, that

9

during the year I've put considerable money into it ; and where the treasure is there shall the heart be also [dead silence]. I've made up my mind, that hurrahing and singing for temperance will make a hypocrite out of a saint, if he don't use money and effort at the same time. I like a good song and a good time as much as anybody, but I can't learn of a single drinking man that they have reformed. At our last meeting there was some good work *started*, by the use of songs and speeches, and you have learned, from the report just presented, how much lasting good they did. Money and work have done the business, my friends ; talk has helped, but alone by itself it's done precious little. This lesson has cost *me* a great deal ; and as a business man, who believes that *every* earthly interest is in some way a business interest, I advise you to learn the same lesson for yourselves before it is too late."

Such a pail of cold water had never before been thrown upon Barton hearts aglow with confidence it struck the leader of the band so forcibly that he rattled off into "Yankee Doodle," to aid the meeting in recovering its spirits ; even after listening to this inspiriting air, however, it was with a wistfulness almost desperate that the audience scanned the countenance of Parson Wedgewell as he stepped to the front of the platform.

" Beloved friends," said the parson, " the result of the past year's work in this portion of the Lord's vineyard has indeed been richly blessed, and I shall ever count it as one of the precious privileges of my life that I have been permitted to take part in it. ['Hurrah for the parson!' shouted a man, who had but a moment before worn a most lugubrious countenance.] I rejoice, not only that I have seen precious sheaves brought to our Lord's granary, but also because I have beheld going into the field those who have heretofore stood idly in the market-place, and because I have beheld the reapers themselves receiving the reward of their labors. They have received souls for their hire, dear friends, and I feel constrained to admit that if each of those who came in at the eleventh hour received as much as us, who have apparently borne the burden and heat of the day, they were fully entitled to it by reason of the greater intelligence and industry which they have displayed. For many years, my dear friends, I have been among you as one sent by the Physician of souls; but it is only within the past year that I have begun to comprehend that the soul may be treated—very often *should* be treated—through the body; and that, though the fervent effectual prayer of the righteous man availeth much, the exercise of that which was made in the likeness and image of God is not to be idle. The mammon of unrighteousness has been made the salvation of many, my dear friends; and it has, I verily believe, guided toward heavenly habitations those who have applied it to the necessities of others. But, dear brethren, the harvest truly is plenteous, but the laborers are few; pray ye, therefore, the Lord of the harvest that he will send forth laborers unto his harvest; but take heed that ye follow the example of him, who, as he commanded us thus to petition the throne of grace, ceased not to labor in the harvest field himself; who fed when he preached, and healed when he exhorted."

Harry Wainright pounded on the floor with his cane, hearing which, Tom Adams brought his enormous hands together with great emphasis, and his example was dutifully followed by the whole of his own family, which filled two short side seats. Father Baguss shouted " Glory to God! " and Deacon Jones ejaculated " That's so! " but the hearers seemed disposed to be critical, although the parson's address had been couched in language almost exclusively Scriptural. While they were engaged in contemplation, however, old Bunley dropped a mellow cough and stepped to the front.

"Ladies and gentlemen," said he, " it's the style in this town, and everywhere else, I suppose, to kick a man when he's down, and then to trample on him. I know *one* man that's been there, and knows all about it. 'Twas his own fault he got there, and there were plenty who told him he ought to get up ; but how kicking and trampling were to help him do it he could never see, and he made up his mind, that folks did as they did because it suited them, not because it was going to do *him* any good. So he's been hating the whole townful for years, and doing all the harm he could, not because he liked doing harm, but because he never got a chance to do anything else. Suddenly, a couple of gentlemen—I won't mention names—came along, and gave the poor fellow a hand, and gave him the first chance he's had in years to believe in human nature at all. And, all this time, everybody else around him was acting in the way that this same poor fellow would have acted himself, if he had wanted to play devil. The same couple of gentle-

men went for a good many other people, and acted
in a way that you read about in novels and the
Bible (but mighty seldom see in town); and those
fellows believe in these two gentlemen, now, but
they hate all the rest of you like poison. I don't
suppose you like it, but truth is truth; you might
as well know what it is."

Several people got up and went out, carrying
very red faces with them; but Fred Macdonald
stood up and clapped his hands, and the Adams
family and Wainright helped him, while the broad
boots of Father Baguss raised a cloud of dust,
which formed quite an aureole about Baguss himself as he got up and remarked:

"Brethren and sisters: Squire Tomple hit the
nail exactly on the head when he said that hollerin'
an' singin' makes a hypocrite of a man if he don't
open his pocket-book. If you don't believe it, remember me. If anybody ever liked his own more'n
I did, he's a curiosity. I don't *hate* money a bit
now, an' I'm not goin' to try to; but the hardest
case I ever got acquainted with was me, Zedekiah
Baguss, when I couldn't dodge it any longer that I
ought to spend money for a feller-critter. I won't
name no names, brethren an' sisters; but if you're

huntin' for any such game, don't go to lookin'
up drunkards until you smell around near home
fust."

"Reputation be blowed higher than a kite!"
exclaimed Captain Crayme, springing to his feet;
"but I've got to say just a word here. Gentlemen,
I'm off my whiskey, and I'm going to stay off; but
I might be drinking yet, and have kept on forever,
for all that any of you that's so pious and temperate
ever cared. But one man thought enough of me
to come and talk to me—talk like a man, and not
preach a sermon; more than that, he not only talked
—which the biggest idiot here might have done just
as well—but he stuck by me, and he brought me
through. Any of you might have done it, but
none of you cared enough for me, and yet I'm a
business man, and I've got some property. How
any *poor* fellow down in the mud is ever to get
up again, in such a place, I don't see; and yet
Barton's as good a town as I ever touch at."

The interest of the meeting was departing, so
were the attendants; but the Reverend Timotheus
Brown limped forward and exclaimed:

" Hear, then, the conclusion of the whole matter:
'Not every one that sayeth Lord, Lord, shall in-

herit the kingdom of heaven, but him that doeth the will of my Father which is in heaven.' There has been a blessed change wrought in this town within a year, and work has done it all. He who taught us to say 'Our Father,' made of every man his brother's keeper, and no amount of talk can undo what He did. A few men in our midst have recognized their duty and have done it, or are doing it; most of them, among them him who addresses you, have learned that the beginning is the hardest part of the work, and that the laborer receives his hire, though never in the way in which he expects it. Much remains to be done, not only in raising the fallen, but in reforming the upright; and, to get a full and fair view of the latter, there is no way so successful as to go to work for others."

Squire Tomple announced that the meeting was still open for remarks; but, no one else availing themselves of the privilege offered, the evening closed with a spirited medley from the brass band. Not every one was silent and dismal, however; as the church emptied, Tomple, Bunley, Crupp, Wedge-well, Brown, and the other pastors came down from the platform, and were met at the foot of the steps by Baguss and Deacon Jones, and there was a general hand-shaking. Tom Adams stood afar off, looking curiously and wistfully at the party, noticing which, Parson Wedgewell danced excitedly up to him, and dragged him into the circle; there Tom received a greeting which somehow educated him, in two or three minutes, to a point far beyond any that his head or heart had previously reached. Then Fred Macdonald, who had intended to avoid any action which might seem to make him one of the " old fellows " of the village, suddenly lost his head in some manner which he could not explain, and hurried off, caught Sam Crayme's arm, and destroyed such reputation as remained to the captain along the river, by bringing the enterprising navigator into such a circle as he had never entered before, but in which he soon found himself as much at home as if he had been born there. Others, too—not many in number, to be sure—but representing most of the soul of the village, straggled timidly up to the group, and were informally admitted to what was not conventionally a love-feast, but approached nearer to one than any formal gathering could have done.

Barton has never since known a monster temperance meeting; but the few righteous men who dwell therein have proved to their own satisfaction, and that of certain one-time wretches, that, in a successful temperance movement, the reform must begin among those who never drink.

www.ingramcontent.com/pod-product-compliance
Lightning Source LLC
Chambersburg PA
CBHW030827270326
41928CB00007B/939